Apad-dharma in The Mahabharata

"The historical background of the present study poses an important, academic question:" How could the Indian society have protected itself against external attacks during the pre-modern period?" Research-based answers to such India-related questions occupy the initial part of this book to which a global dimension has been added by digging deep into Mahabharata's innumerable stories. Results of innovative investigations into the general question "How to face calamities at personal, state, and global levels", are presented here in terms of a modern, scientific framework, and expressed in a non-denominational terminology, relevant to the problems of the 21st century. Readers from all parts of the world can get a strong message of social responsibility from this book, and accordingly make their contribution to the cause of world peace.

Other Books by the Same Author

1. The Social Role of the Gita: How and Why
2. The Social Message of the Gita Symbolized as Lokasamgraha
3. तुलसी रामायण - जगमंगल-परायण
4. मानस एवं गीता - लोकमंगल-गुम्फिता
5. लोकसंग्रहसन्देशः
6. The Gita and Tulsi-Ramayana : Their Common Call for the Good of All
7. Selections from the Mahabharata
8. The Gita for the 21st Century
9. छात्रोपयोगी भगवद्गीता
10. श्रीमद्भागवत का ज्ञान
11. The World Peace Agenda

Apad-dharma *in* The Mahabharata

How to Face Calamities at Personal, State, and Global Levels

SATYA P. AGARWAL
Ph.D. (UC, Berkeley)
Formerly, Chief Technical Adviser,
Specialized Agency (ILO) of the United Nations
and Visiting Scholar,
University of California, Berkeley

New Age Books

ISBN: 978-81-7822-361-2

First Indian Edition: Delhi, 2010

Published by
NEW AGE BOOKS
A-44, Naraina Industrial Area, Phase-I
New Delhi 110 028 (INDIA)
Email: nab@vsnl.in
Website: www.newagebooksindia.com

Distributors
Urmila Agarwal
11293 Ridermark Row
Columbia MD 21044
Tel.: USA-410-997-7175
Email: ishamaya@crols.com

Printed in India
at Shri Jainendra Press
A-45, Naraina Phase-I, New Delhi 110 028

To My Parents
who taught me
That social responsibility
And world peace promotion
go together

Contents

Humble Submission
Regarding the Sanskrit Text

The author asks for forgiveness from the Mahabharata-specialists for not having used the critical edition of the epic. Due to his life-long association with the Editor of Gita Press, Gorakhpur, he has at his finger-tips, the messages of social responsibility, extracted from their six-volume (unabridged) version, and he feels that the use of the critical edition would probably have no significant impact on these messages.

Secondly, the author asks for forgiveness from specialists in linguistics for not having strictly adhered to all the rules of transliteration. Similarly, he has not given a word-for-word translation of the selected verses. He feels that the purpose of this book will be better served by giving priority to the convenience of general readers.

Preface

The literal meaning of the Sanskrit word "Apad-dharma" is "dharma appropriate at the time of calamity". The Mahabharata's use of this expression implies that, in the opinion of the author of this epic, the traditional varnashrama-dharma would not prove to be strong enough to protect the society, if and when there is a calamity (say, an attack from outside). Therefore, Vedic scholars ought to have welcomed the messages of Apad-dharma when the society was actually attacked by external forces during the pre-modern period. However, it is a sad, historical fact that Apad-dharma of the Mahabharata was neglected by traditional scholars, not only before external attacks took place, but also after such attacks had taken place. Instead of welcoming Apad-dharma, the traditional scholars gave to common people, an anti-Mahabharata message: "Don't keep the Mahabharata in your house because, if you do, then there will be Mahabharata-like war in your house". But the warrelated text of the Mahabharata is confined to the first nine Parvas only - the remaining nine Parvas are devoted to Shanti (i.e. peace) and they contain more shlokas than the first nine Parvas. The Apad-dharma text belongs to Shanti-Parva (which is Parva No. 12 and is the longest Parva in the entire epic). Therefore, the real reasons for the neglect of Apad-dharma have never been specified.

While I was searching for those reasons, I saw (in my dream) the full text, clearly written on a screen, of a long dialogue between two immortal scholars who spoke to each other, in the traditionally courteous manner, on six different dates, spread over a time span of 2100 years. The first scholar (referred to as Scholar V) is a traditional Vedic Scholar (who, for this dialogue, can also be called Varnashrama-dharma scholar). The second scholar (referred to as Scholar A) is an Apad-dharma scholar. The six different dates of the screen dialogue are: (a) 2000 years ago, (b) 1000 years ago, (c) 500 years ago, (d) 200 years ago, (e) now, and (f) 100 years in the future. The full text of the six part dialogue (which I saw on the screen), is reproduced below.

Dialogue No. 1 (2000 years ago)

Scholar A. Namastey. You have rendered a great social service by teaching all the people about dharma. May I refer to this dharma as "peace time dharma"?

Scholar V. Namastey. I am happy to hear appreciative words spoken by you about our teaching activities. But why do you want to use the expression "peace time dharma" ?

Scholar A. Because it seems to me that, some time in the future, if our country is attacked from outside, then the Varnashrama-dharma that you are teaching, will not prove to be strong enough to protect the society. The dharma that will ensure protection of the society against any calamity is called "Apad-dharma". So "peace time dharma" would be a correct expression for Varnashrama-dharma.

Scholar V. It seems to me that you are a pessimist. Why do you imagine that our country will ever be attacked from outside? Our dharma has taught people not to attack any outsider. So why should we unnecessarily create fear in the minds of people that we will be attacked ?

Scholar A. I too am not in favor of creating fear in the minds of people. So please excuse me for having suggested the use of the expression "peace time dharma", even before any attack from outside takes place. Namastey.

Dialogue No. 2 (1000 years ago)

Scholar A. Namastey. You may recall that I wanted to use the expression "peace time dharma" when I spoke to you 1000 years ago, but you did not agree, saying that it will unnecessarily create fear in the minds of people.

Scholar V. Namastey. Yes, I remember that.

Scholar A. Can you change your mind now, because our country has actually been attacked from outside, and the Varnashrama-dharma that you taught proved to be weak, in the face of that calamity.

Scholar V. Failure on one or two occasions in a thousand years need not cause any alarm. So I don't feel like changing the view that I expressed 1000 years ago.

Scholar A. I don't want to prolong the discussion. Namastey.

Dialogue No. 3 (500 years ago).

Scholar A. Namastey. Since I spoke to you 500 years ago, our country has been attacked from outside several times, and the weakness of Varnashrama-dharma has been exposed again and again, in the face of those attacks. Can you please change your mind now and teach people Apad-dharma as a means of protection against future attacks?

Scholar V. Namastey. You are becoming impatient. A few more failures in 500 years need not be taken so seriously. Therefore, I still don't feel like changing my earlier opinion.

Scholar A. Although I feel that you are delaying the urgently - needed protective action for the society, I won't press the point further. Namastey.

Dialogue No. 4 (200 years ago)

Scholar A. Namastey. Tragic failures of the last 300 years must have shaken your old confidence. So I hope you will now agree to teach people Apad-dharma (instead of Varnashrama-dharma), to ensure the protection of the society against future attacks.

Scholar V. Namastey. Yes, we have now realised that we did not provide for adequate protection against external attacks. But we will change the dharma gradually, to the extent necessary, rather than adopt Apad-dharma in its entirety. So please wait and see, and postpone the idea of using the expression "peace time dharma".

Scholar A. I will wait. Namastey.

Dialogue No. 5 (Now)

Scholar A. Namastey. I have waited 200 years. I hope you have now realised that unsystematic (patch work) ways of strengthening Varnashrama-dharma can not ensure full protection of the society against external attacks. That will be possible only if the need to teach Apad-dharma as a supplemental dharma is recognized.

Scholar V. Namastey. I fully agree to what you say.

Scholar A. I am happy that, by mutual agreement, we can now provide for full protection of the society against external attacks. Namastey.

Dialogue No. 6 (100 years in the future)

Scholar A. Namastey. One hundred years ago, we agreed on a common approach. Has this made any impact on the attackers?

Scholar V. Namastey. Yes, the attackers telephoned and said that, after getting the news of the agreement between us, they decided to postpone the attack.

Scholar A. Very good. Let us maintain the agreement, because that ensures our protection.

Scholar V. I agree. Namastey.

Here ends the screen dialogue, which seems to me as conveying, in a unique way, three messages about Apad-dharma and the traditional Varnashrama-dharma –

(i) That Apad-dharma was neglected by traditional scholars for a very long time

(ii) That the Indian society suffered heavily due to external attacks because some features of Varnashrama-dharma made the society vulnerable

(iii) As soon as Apad-dharma is taught to the Indian society, as a supplement to Varnashrama-dharma, then the society will become capable of facing external attacks successfully.

This book presents, for the first time, a consolidated, easy-to-read version of the messages of Apad-dharma, expressed in a non-denominational terminology. I am confident that readers will find these messages to have universal applicability, as well as considerable flexibility which can make them relevant to the problems of the 21st century. Such relevance of ancient messages to today's conditions will be found to exist, in-spite of the availability of assistance from police, army, and other protective agencies, to citizens of different countries in modern times.

SATYA P. AGARWAL

Acknowledgements

Although the drafting of this book was essentially a family - supported research project, valuable feedback (at the time of finalization of the draft) came informally from close friends. Dr. Rajan Narayanan organized a series of talks on this book, at Shri Shiva Vishnu Temple, and scholars providing feedback (other than Dr. Narayanan himself) included Dr. Sham Narula, Dr. Dinesh Sinha, Dr. R. S. Dwivedi, Dr. Pooran and Kusum Shukla, Dr. Gopal Dorai, Madanmohan and Anju Khanna, Rakshpal and Santosh Aggarwal; Jaishriben and Ila Desai. My special thanks to all of them.

Within my own family or svajanam (in the language of the Mahabharata), my wife Urmila's role has been unique - she read the manuscript and gave very useful comments. She also envisaged the cover design (which was accordingly finalized by the publishers' artist). Technical and moral support came from all the members of the family viz. Nishkam, Kokila, Seema, David, Isha, Kiran, Priya, and Maya. Close relatives who rendered valuable help include Shri Harish Kashyap, M. M. Agarwal, Arun and Ritu Gupta, Veena and Anil Kumar, Manju and Dhanendra Kumar, Renu Mital, Dr. K. M. Mital, Shri Gulab Khandelwal, Rakesh and Alka Mital, Savita and Anil Agarwal, and Abhay Bhushan. To all of them as well as to many others who rendered help but whose names are not specifically mentioned (in order to keep this list short), I express my sincere thankfulness.

SATYA P. AGARWAL

Columbia, Maryland

15 April, 2009

Part I

Based on Stories from Shastras

Part I

Based on Stories from Shanti Parva

CHAPTER 1

Shanti Parva and Apad-dharma Inspiring New Studies on the Mahabharata

1.1 The Mahabharata text which is the longest literary composition of the ancient world, has been studied by scholars from various perspectives. Broadly speaking, while the first half of this text describes in detail the terrible war that took place between the Pandavas and the Kauravas, the second half discusses, in greater detail, how future wars can be prevented. Due to one reason or the other, most of the Mahabharata studies published prior to 9/11/2001 concentrated attention on the first half of the text, that is, presented the Mahabharata as "a book of war". However, recent studies have shifted attention from the first to the second half of the text, that is, viewed the Mahabharata as "a book of peace".

1.2 A simple explanation for such divergent views about the same text is, that the Mahabarata has a vast ocean-like coverage, as is clear from its own famous declaration:

> धर्मे चार्थे च कामे च मोक्षे च भरतर्षभ।
> यदिहास्ति तदन्यत्र यन्नेहास्ति न कुत्रचित्॥ 18.5.50
>
> *dharme carthe ca kame ca mokse ca bharatarsabha*
> *yadihasti tadanyatra yannehasti na kutracit*
>
> *—18.5.50*

Simple meaning—Vaishampayana declares in the last chapter of the Mahabharata, "On the topics of dharma, artha, kama, and moksa (*i.e.* the four goals of life), what you find in this book may be found elsewhere, but whatever is not found here, you will not be able to find anywhere else".

1.3 Since we shall frequently refer to different parts of the Mahabharata (called "Parva"), it will be useful to provide, at the outset, the Sanskrit title of each of the eighteen Parvas, together with brief indicators of the contents thereof:

(i) *Adi Parva* (*i.e.* common ancestors of both the Pandavas and the Kauravas of whom Shakuntala is perhaps the most famous. Origin of the conflict between the two groups of cousins)

(ii) *Sabha Parva* (*i.e.* Assemblies where gambling took place, aggravating the conflict)

(iii) *Vana Parva* (*i.e.* Pandavas' stay in the forest for twelve years. Here Rishis visit them and tell great stories (including the story of Savitri, to which we will refer in Chapter Eight. Towards the end of the Parva, Yudhisthira faces a calamity to which we shall refer in Chapter Nine)

(iv) *Virata Parva* (*i.e.* Pandavas' stay in disguise at king Virata's court. End of the 13th year. How Pandavas saved king Virata from calamity)

(v) *Udyoga Parva* (*i.e.* Preparations for war)

(vi) *Bhisma Parva* (*i.e.* Ten days of the war when Bhisma led the Kauravas. This Parva contains Bhagavad Gita)

(vii) *Drona Parva* (*i.e.* Five days of the war when Drona led the Kauravas)

(viii) *Karna Parva* (*i.e.* Two days of the war when Karna led the Kauravas)

(ix) *Salya Parva* (*i.e.* One day of the war when Salya led the Kauravas. Duryodhana's death, marking the end of the war)

(x) *Sauptika Parva* (*i.e.* Treacherously killing people while they were asleep)

(xi) *Stri Parva* (*i.e.* Grief-stricken widows)

(*xii*) *Shanti Parva* (*i.e.* Long dialogue between Bhisma and Yudhisthira relating to shanti *i.e.* Peace. One of the three sections of Shanti Parva is called "Apad-dharma" which can be translated as "How to face calamities")

(*xiii*) *Anusasana Parva* (*i.e.* continuation of Shanti Parva)

(*xiv*) *Asvamedha Parva* (*i.e.* Lord Krishna finally leaves the Pandavas and goes to Dwaraka. Before leaving, he teaches Anu Gita, as a follow up of Bhagavad Gita)

(*xv*) *Asramavasika Parva* (*i.e.* Dhritarastra's last days in the forest)

(*xvi*) *Mausala Parva* (*i.e.* Self-destruction by Yadavas in Dwaraka. Shanti Parva had given a warning 36 years in advance)

(*xvii*) *Mahaprasthanika Parva* (*i.e.* Pandavas' final journey on foot towards heaven. Yudhisthira's declaration about not abandoning any member of the group that had walked with him, even for the sake of heaven)

(*xviii*) *Svargarohana Parva* (*i.e.* Pandavas' arrival in heaven. Happy ending of the Mahabharata, for every one)

1.4 *New studies inspired by Shanti Parva:* Among the new studies based on the Mahabharata, we want to draw attention to those that have been recently inspired by Shanti Parva. In 2002, the author of this book wrote "Selections from the Mahabharata—Reaffirming Gita's call for the Good of All".[1] The Sanskrit word for the good of all is "lokasamgraha", and Shanti Parva made it possible to explain lokasamgraha's ten aspects (*i.e.* elaboration of Bhagavad Gita's ideas).

1.5 In 2006, Sitansu S. Chakravarti wrote "Ethics in the Mahabharatha— A Philosophical Inquiry for Today." While discussing the central philosophy of the Mahabharata, this book pays special attention to Bhagavad Gita, and concludes that "the dominant mood of the Mahabharata is peace".[2]

1.6 In 2007, the author of the present book wrote "The World Peace Agenda - Based on Shanti Parva of the Mahabharata".[3] This book formulated a peace initiative for which the guiding principle was:

जघन्यमाहुर्विजयं युद्धेन 12.94.1

jaghanyamahurvijayam yuddhena

—12.94.1

Simple meaning—Wars cannot provide a satisfactory solution to any dispute.

The peace initiative had three components, which corresponded to the three sections of Shanti Parva:

(i) Raja-dharma

(ii) Apad-dharma (For purposes of interpretation, this section was assigned no. (iii))

(iii) Moksa-dharma

Raja-dharma was interpreted to specify what governments could do to promote the cause of world peace. Similarly, Moksa-dharma was interpreted to specify what religious leaders could do to promote the cause of world peace. Finally, Apad-dharma was interpreted to give the message that the task of establishing world peace should not be restricted to be done by governments and religious leaders only—rather every citizen of the world should also make a contribution (like emergency measures).

Under-utilization of Apad-dharma

1.7 Apad-dharma explains how to face calamities at three levels, viz. *(a)* individual, *(b)* state, and *(c)* global. Out of these, only the global component was utilized by "The World Peace Agenda" referred to above. The need to have complete coverage of Apad-dharma in a single book has therefore been felt. Hence the idea of writing the present book (which will also include the part utilized by "The World Peace Agenda").

The Purpose of the Book

1.8 The purpose of the present book is to make available to all the citizens of the world, the wisdom of the Mahabharata on a topic of great importance in the 21st century, viz. how to face calamities at different levels.

How Apad-dharma Became a Part of the Mahabharata-text

1.9 Apad-dharma is a section of Shanti Parva *(i.e.* Parva No. 12). The great Kaurava leader, Bhisma had fallen down in the battlefield in Parva No. 6, but he did not die because he had the yogic power to determine the exact timing of his passing away. The war ended in Parva No. 9. After the war was over, although Yudhisthira was the winner, he felt unhappy that so many lives of near and dear ones were lost. He then received advice from several great personalities of the Mahabharata, including Vyasa and Lord Krishna. However, Lord Krishna felt that Yudhisthira should still receive a sort of training to be imparted by Bhisma (who was still alive).

1.10 But how did Bhisma acquire the status of a great teacher like Vyasa and Lord Krishna? His conduct in the early part of the Mahabharata was not free from blemish. In Shanti Parva, when Lord Krishna suggested to Bhisma that he may please answer Yudhisthira's questions, Bhisma himself narrated his weaknesses-

दौर्बल्यात् सज्जते वाङ् मे स कथं वक्तुमुत्सहे ।
किं चाहमभिधास्यामि वाक्यं ते तव संन्निधौ ॥ 12.52.9

daurbalyat sajjate van me sa katham vaktumutsahe
kim cahamabhidhasyami vakyam te tava samnnidhau
—12.52.9

Simple meaning—Bhisma said to Lord Krishna, "I feel very weak now, and I am aware of my earlier weaknesses too. Furthermore, in your presence, what authority do I have to answer Yudhisthira's questions?"

But Lord Krishna wanted Bhisma to get rid of all his weaknesses, and to become a great teacher:

आधेयं तु मया भूयो यशस्तव महाद्युते।
ततो मे विपुला बुद्धिस्त्वयि भीष्म समर्पिता ॥ 12.54.27

adheyam tu maya bhuyo yasastava mahadyute
tato me vipula budhistvayi bhisma samarpita
—12.54.27

Simple meaning—Lord Krishna said to Bhisma, "I want that you should become a well-known teacher. For this purpose, I am bestowing on you "vipula buddhi" i.e. "broad-mindedness".

> यच्च त्वं वक्ष्यसे भीष्म पाण्डवायानुपृच्छते।
> वेदप्रवाद इव ते स्थास्यते वसुधातले ॥ 12.54.29
>
> *yacca tvam vaksyase bhisma pandavayanupricchate*
> *vedapravada iva te sthasyate vasudhatale*
>
> —*12.54.29*

Simple meaning—Lord Krishna added, "Whatever reply you will give to Yudhisthira, in response to his questions, that will be recognized as valid as the Vedas."

1.11 Shanti Parva is the longest Parva in the Mahabharata, and when combined with Anusasana Parva (which is a continuation of Shanti Parva), it accounts for more than one-fourth of the epic. The style of Shanti Parva is, using a story to give a message. In some of the stories, animals have a role as characters. Such stories need to be suitably interpreted so as to be of use to human beings.

1.12 As already mentioned in para 1.9, Apad-dharma is a section of Shanti Parva. It has forty three chapters. However, some of the stories of Raja-dharma and Moksa-dharma also deal with the question "How to face calamities". So, for our purpose, we make use of "extended Apad-dharma" (although the term "extended" is not specifically mentioned in the title of this book).

1.13 We want to stress that messages that we have derived from Apad-dharma are non-denominational, and have universal applicability. Readers will notice that, although the Mahabharata is an ancient text, its messages are relevant even today, and deserve to be read with an open mind.

Plan of the Book

1.14 The book is divided into three parts. Part I is based on stories from Shanti Parva and Anusasana Parva—five stories have been selected so as to have at least one story relating to each of the three levels specified in para 1.7. Part II is based on stories from Parvas other than Shanti Parva and Anusasana Parva *i.e.* stories that deal with the question "How to face calamities". For Part II also, five stories have been selected, four relating to individual level calamities, and one relating to state level calamity. (No story relating to global level calamity is available from Parvas other than Shanti Parva). Finally, Part III presents a summary of Parts I, and II, and concluding remarks.

Chapter 2

Sources of Strength for Facing Calamities at Different Levels

2.1 Messages of Apad-dharma, as in Shanti Parva as a whole, are given mainly with the help of stories. Most of the stories are related to calamities at the individual level, for example, risk to a person's life. Some of the stories refer to calamity at the state level. In the opinion of the Mahabharata, internal conflicts, rather than external forces, are likely to contribute more to calamities at the state level. Finally, one story considers "too much violence" as a calamity at the global level. But that story is narrated twice in Shanti Parva, perhaps giving a message that Vyasa attached special significance to global level calamity.

2.2 The overall message of Apad-dharma is that every calamity should be faced intelligently, avoiding a foolhardy approach. Strength of head and heart is given precedence over physical strength, without undervaluing the latter. In fact, the following ten sources of strength constitute the general framework out of which the applicability of a particular source to a specific calamity depends on a case-by-case assessment:

(i) Heart हृदय (hridaya)

(ii) Prayer प्रार्थना (prarthana)

(iii) Self-purification आत्म शुद्धि (atmasuddhi)

(iv) Joint effort संघात (sanghata)

(v) Unbreakable relationship भेदमुक्ति (bhedamukti)

(vi) Intellect बुद्धि (buddhi)

(vii) Vocal skill वाक् (vak)

(viii) Skill in action कर्मकौशल (karmakausala)

(ix) Change of priorities प्राथमिकता परिवर्तन (prathamikata parivartana)

(x) Steadfastness धृति (dhriti)

We now explain these sources of strength, one by one

2.3 Heart हृदय (hridaya)

Apad-dharma says that a faint-hearted person who starts crying at the arrival of a calamity, is inherently incapable of facing that calamity.

आपदास्पदकाले तु विलाप: किं करिष्यति। 12.153.34
नैव वाष्पविमोक्षेण न वा श्वासकृते न च।
न च दीर्घरुदितेन तस्माद् दैन्यभावं त्यजेत्।। 12.153.77

apadaspadakale tu vilapah kim karisyati
—12.153.34

naiva vaspavimoksena na va svasakrite na ca
na ca dirgharuditena tasmad dainyabhavan tyajet
—12.153.77

Simple meaning—When a calamity occurs, how will lamentation help you to face it? Neither the shedding of tears, nor the drawing of long sighs, nor copious crying - none of these is of any use. You need to give up your faint-heartedness, as the first step, that is a 'must', to be strong enough at heart, to meet the challenge.

आपत्काले तनुं त्यक्तुं मनोभारो विशेषत:।
मनोबलं तु समास्थाय जीवितव्यं सदा भवेत् ॥
जीवन् पुण्यमवाप्नोति पुरुषो भद्रमश्नुते ॥ 12.141.101

apatkale tanum tyaktum manobharo visesatah
manobalam tu samasthaya jivitavyam sada bhavet
jivan punayamavapnoti puruso bhadramasnute

—12.141.101

Simple meaning—If you lose heart, you succumb to the calamity even before it strikes you. You might even commit suicide. Therefore don't let will power abandon you—that will keep you alive by giving you hope that if you remain alive, you can do good deeds in due course of time.

पीडितस्य किमद्वारमुत्पथो विधृतस्य च । 12.130.22
अद्वारतः प्रद्रवति हृदयेनापराजितः ॥ 12.130.14
उपायधर्ममाचरेत् हृदयेनापराजितः ॥ 12.130.13

piditasya kimadvaramutpatho vidhritasya ca

—12.130.22

advaratah pradravati hridayenaparajitah

—12.130.14

upayadharmamacaret hridayenaparajitah

—12.130.13

Simple meaning—Don't feel that there is no hope of success. At this early stage, you cannot possibly identify the door to safety. But a brave heart will give you hope that a "door of no-door" does exist, although you cannot see it. Your immediate response should be to keep the urge to make effort.

2.4 Prayer प्रार्थना (prarthana)

The purpose underlying prayer, according to Apad-dharma, is not to ask for victory, but rather to ask for strength needed to face the calamity.

न कांक्षे विजयं कृष्ण।
कांक्षे शक्तिं यत्नार्थाय ॥ 13.145.166

na kankse vijayam krishna
kankse saktim yatnarthaya

—13.145.166

Simple meaning—O God, my prayer is not to ask for easy victory (handed over to me without any effort on my part), rather I ask for strength so that I can put in my best effort.

"Strength" includes physical and mental strength for which Shanti Parva recommends the practice of yoga, pranayama and meditation, and consumption of healthy vegetarian food.[1]

2.5 Self-purification आत्मशुद्धि (atmasuddhi)

The role of self-purification is particularly important if one's own mistakes have contributed to the occurrence of the calamity.

आपदो द्विविधाः पार्थ स्वकृता यदि वान्यतः।
स्वकृतापद्मुक्तिः खलु ह्यात्मशुद्ध्या तु प्राप्तव्या ॥ 12.81.13

apado dvividhah partha svakrita yadi vanyatah
svakritapadmuktih khalu hyatmasuddhya tu praptavya
—12.81.13

Simple meaning—Quite often, one's own mistakes have contributed to the occurrence of the calamity. In such cases, the process of facing the calamity successfully, depends largely on one's willingness to rectify those mistakes.

Apad-dharma points out that the process of self-purification consists of two steps:

(i) Repentance, and strengthening of self-discipline

(ii) Determination that old mistakes will not be repeated, and also that even unpleasant action will be gladly undertaken, if needed to rectify those mistakes.

The importance of self-purification (or reform)is brought out in Gautami's story (in chapter Three)

विकर्मणा तप्यमानः पापाद् विपरिमुच्यते।
नैतत् कार्यं पुनरिति द्वितीयात् परिमुच्यते॥ 12.152.23
कृत्वा पापं पूर्वमबुद्धिपूर्वं
पुण्यानि चेत्कुरुते बुद्धिपूर्वं

स तत् पापं नुदते कर्मशीलो
वासो यथा मलिनं क्षारयुक्तम् ॥ 12.152.34

vikarmana tapyamanah papad viparimucyate
naitat karyam punariti dvitiyat parimucyate
—12.152.23

kritva papam purvamabuddhipurvam
punyani cetkurute buddhipurvam
sa tat papam nudate karmasilo
vaso yatha malinam ksarayuktam
—12.152.34

Simple meaning—The first step to undo the effect of one's old mistakes is to acknowledge that mistakes were indeed committed. The second step is to take a firm decision that old mistakes will not be repeated.

Taking of 'rectifying action' is the main ingredient of the process of self-purification. Such action can be compared to the use of soap that removes dirt from clothes.

2.6 Joint effort संघात (sanghata)

Apad-dharma says that if the calamity to a state is caused by several enemies' joint aggression, then two crucial pieces of advice are:

अपर्याप्तमापद्मुक्त्यै चेदेकेन कृतो यत्नः।
न बहूनभियुंजीत यौगपद्येन शात्रवान् ॥ 12.103.36

aparyaptamapadmuktyai cedekena krito yatnah
na bahunabhiyunjita yaugapadyena satravan
—12.103.36

Simple meaning—(i) It is not advisable to face the calamity "alone".

(ii) It is not advisable to face several enemies, all at the same time.

Three remedial steps, needed to implement the above-mentioned pieces of advice, are:

सहायान् सततं कुर्याद् लोकचित्तग्रहे रतान्। 12.57.25

न पतत्यरिभिर्ग्रस्तः पतितश्चावतिष्ठते ॥ 12.57.28

sahayan satatam kuryad lokacittagrahe ratan

—12.57.25

na patatyaribhirgrastah patitascavatisthate

—12.57.28

Simple meaning—(iii) In order to face the calamity successfully, the state should look for supporters (who should be equally interested in doing good to people).

Strengthened by their support, the state cannot be overcome by enemies, and even if the state suffers setback temporarily, it will be able to recover, and regain adequate strength needed to face the calamity.

नैतान्येकेन शक्यानि सातत्येनानुवीक्षितुम् ।
तेषु सर्वं प्रतिष्ठाप्य संघातबलं वर्धयेत् ॥ 12.93.26

naitanyekena sakyani satatyenanuviksitum
tesu sarvam pratisthapya sanghatabalam vardhayet

—12.93.26

Simple meaning—(iv) Since any single member of the support group cannot possibly be expected to take full responsibility for all that needs to be done, the efficiency of joint effort should be increased by delegating responsibility to different members of the support group.

ज्ञानिना सन्निकृष्टस्य शत्रोरपि परिग्रहः ।
कार्य इत्याहुराचार्या यथा कृतं भूषिकेण ॥ 12.138.45

jnanina sannikristasya satrorapi parigrahah
karya ityahuracarya yatha kritam musikena

—12.138.45

Simple meaning—(v) In order to strengthen oneself, and to weaken the enemies at the same time, the state should try to make peace with one of the enemies. This piece of advice has been given by famous scholars, and its practical implementation is illustrated in Apad-dharma through the story of a wise mouse who protected himself, although he had three enemies.

(This story is summarized in chapter Five of this book. Although this story primarily relates to individual level calamity, its message can be applied to state level calamity also.)

2.7 The suggestion to make peace with the enemy is particularly mentioned by Apad-dharma when the enemy is stronger than oneself (*i.e.* the state or individual facing aggression):

प्रत्युत्पन्नमतिः कुयात् शत्रोः परिग्रहं संध्या ।
तस्माद् वैरं न कुर्वीत दुर्बलो बलवत्तरैः ॥
तथानागतविधाता स्वकृतामापदां हरेत् ॥ 12.157.9

pratyutpannamatih kuryat satroh parigraham sandhya
tasmad vairam na kurvita durbalo balavattaraih
tathanagatavidhata svakritamapadam haret
—12.157.9

Simple meaning—Apad-dharma recommends a preventive approach that does not wait for the calamity to occur. If an enemy is stronger than the state itself, then the possibility of aggression from that enemy should be averted by entering into a peace treaty therewith, as much in advance as possible, as a farsighted policy. The expression 'anagatavidhata' means that this is done much before the problem arises. Similarly, the expression 'pratyutpannamati' means that the peace treaty with the strong enemy is accomplished, if not in advance, then in any case before the calamity occurs. A comparative assessment of one's own strength, and that of the enemy, is therefore necessary. The role of 'sanghata' (joint effort) is to alter the situation in one's favour. Apad-dharma stresses the need to avoid an "unequal battle in which one is bound to lose" (that would be like committing suicide)

2.8 Unbreakable relationship भेदमुक्ति (bhedamukti)

Apad-dharma says that the inherent strength of a state depends on the nature of relationship that exists among important subgroups that together sustain the state, and are responsible for its protection against aggression.

आभ्यन्तरं भयं रक्ष्यमसारं बाह्यतो भयम्।
आभ्यन्तरं भयं राजन् सद्यो मूलानि कृन्तति ॥ 12.107.28

abhyantaram bhayam raksyamasaram bahyato bhayam
abhyantaram bhayan rajan sadyo mulani krintati
—12.107.28

Simple meaning—The calamity that a state faces, occurs more often due to internal problems, as compared to external causes. In fact, if internal problems are not taken care of, then they cut the roots and make the entire structure shaky, thus creating conditions which can be exploited by external forces.

भेदमूलो विनाशो हि गणानामुपलक्षये । 12.107.8
भेदे गणा विनेशुर्हि भिन्नास्तु सुजया परैः ॥ 12.107.14

bhedamulo vinaso hi gananamupalaksaye
—12.107.8

bhede gana vinesurhi bhinnastu sujaya paraih
—12.107.14

Simple meaning—The main cause of destruction of a state, or of a group of neighboring states, is 'lack of unity or team spirit'. Lack of harmonious relationship weakens the group, and that makes it an easy prey for the invaders.

भेदाच्चैव प्रदानाच्च भिद्यन्ते रिपुभिर्गणाः ।
तस्मात् संघातमेवाहुर्गणानां शरणं महत् ॥ 12.107.31
संघातबलमजेयं प्रासव्या तेनापद्मुक्तिः ।
भेदमूलो विनाशो हि भेदमुक्त्या त्वापद्मुक्तिः ॥ 12.107.32

bhedaccaiva pradanacca bhidyante ripubhirganah
tasmat sanghatamevahurgananam saranam mahat
—12.107.31

sanghatabalamajeyam praptavya tenapadmuktih
bhedamulo vinaso hi bhedamuktya tvapadmuktih
—12.107.32

Simple meaning—The harmonious relationship within a state or a group of states has to be unbreakable and unbribable—

and that makes the state or the group of states 'unconquerable'. That is why 'bhedamukti' (unbreakable relationship) and 'apadmukti' (calamity-free existence) are practically synonymous expressions in Apad-dharma. More on this in Chapter Six of this book.

2.9 Intellect बुद्धि (buddhi)

Apad-dharma uses the expressions 'buddhi', 'prajna' and 'medha' as practically interchangeable (and, in the present context, the English word 'intellect' covers all of them). This source of strength is given special recognition, in the context of facing calamities at all levels.

उद्धरेद् दीनमात्मानं संव्यवस्य: स्वया धिया । 12.130.7
ये तु बुद्ध्या हि बलिनस्ते भवन्ति बलीयस: ॥ 12.156.12
संघातबलसाधनं बुद्धिसाहाय्यं संज्ञितम् ॥ 12.82.33

uddhared dinamatmanam samvyavasyah svaya dhiya
—12.130.7

ye tu buddhya hi balinaste bhavanti baliyasah
—12.156.12

sanghatabalasadhanam buddhisahayyam sanjnitam
—12.82.33

Simple meaning—Use the intellect of the group (*i.e.* coordinated intellect of all the supporters) to face the calamity. Right intellect is the main source of strength for this purpose, and therefore, supporters who give the right advice contribute the most to the effectiveness of joint effort.

उपलभ्य मतिं शुद्धामरिमित्रान्तरं तथा ।
संधिविग्रहकालौ च मोक्षोपायस्तथैव च ॥ 12.138.214

upalabhya matim suddhamarimitrantaram tatha
sandhivigrahakalau ca moksopayastathaiva ca
—12.138.214

Simple meaning—Right intellect studies the situation scientifically—comparative strength of both sides in the conflict, how to negotiate a peace treaty if it is in one's interest, etc.—and then works out the best possible plan for success (which may include a peace treaty with the enemy).

2.10 Illustrative stories (or historical narratives) occur throughout the Mahabharata - text, showing how intelligent persons faced calamities successfully. For example, in the first Parva (*i.e.* Adi - Parva) itself, it is described in detail how Shakuntala protected her marriage and her son, because she made full use of her 'prajna' (intellect). Chapter Ten of this book summarizes Shakuntala's eventful life, but two important messages that she gave to mankind are contained in the following shloka.

नरेष्वापद्पतितेषु भार्या करोति रक्षणम् ।
नारीष्वापद्पतितासु प्रज्ञा करोति रक्षणम् ॥ 13.145.109

naresvapadpatitesu bharya karoti raksanam
narisvapadpatitasu prajna karoti raksanam
—13.145.109

Simple meaning—What protects a person, when he or she is face-to-face with calamity? Shakuntala's life provides memorable answers: *(a)* When a man is in calamity, his wife protects him. *(b)* When a woman is in calamity, her intellect protects her.

2.11 Apad-dharma's own story about the application of intellect for achieving calamity-free existence, uses a 'mouse' as the main character, the underlying message being that if a mouse can do this, then why not a human being. This story is summarized in Chapter Five of this book, but one shloka (referring to prajna) is given here too.

मूषिकः सर्वतो रुद्धः सर्वत्र भयदर्शनः । 12.138.35
न धर्मकुशलः प्राज्ञः सम्मोहं गन्तुमर्हति ॥ 12.138.38

musikah sarvato ruddhah sarvatra bhayadarsanah
—12.138.35

na dharmakusalah prajnah sammoham gantumarhati
—12.138.38

Simple meaning—The mouse had three enemies who threatened him, all at once. But the mouse made full use of his prajna (intellect) and was able to protect himself.

2.12 Shanti Parva's story relating to calamity at the global level, has, as its main character, a brilliant young scholar, whose name was 'Medhavi', and it is pointed out, in the beginning of that story, that his name (meaning 'intelligent') correctly epitomized the young man who was 'intelligent'.

> द्विजातेः कस्यचित् पार्थ स्वाध्यायनिरतस्य वै ।
> बभूव पुत्रो मेधावी मेधावी नाम नामतः ॥ 12.175.3
> *dvijateh kasyacit partha svadhyayaniratasya vai*
> *babhuva putro medhavi medhavi nama namatah*
> *—12.175.3*

Simple meaning—There was a brahmin who used to study ancient scriptures. He got a son whom he gave the name 'Medhavi'—the son was intelligent (and the word 'Medhavi' also means 'intelligent').

Medhavi's story is summarized in Chapter Seven of this book.

2.13 Vocal skill वाक् (vak)

Since Shanti Parva's overall recommendation is to face calamities peacefully, the problems are to be resolved in conference halls, and not on the battlefield. Therefore, vocal skills are very important. One of the important stories of Anusasana Parva relates to a non-violent scholar who won over a violent monster by making full use of his vocal skills. This story is summarized in Chapter Four of this book, but the first shloka (specifically referring to his vocal skill) is given here.

> कश्चिद् वाग्बुद्धिसम्पन्नो ब्राह्मणो विजने वने।
> गृहीतः कृच्छ्रमापन्नो रक्षसा भक्षयिष्यता ॥ 13.124.5
> *kascid vagbuddhisampanno brahmano vijane vane*
> *grihitah kricchramapanno raksasa bhaksayisyata*
> *—13.124.5*

Simple meaning—A certain scholar, endowed with vocal skill as well as intelligence, fell into distress, because he was seized in a lone forest by a monster who wanted to eat him up. (At the end of the story, they became friends.)

2.14 Shanti Parva says that the expression 'vocal skill' needs to be understood in a comprehensive sense.

नाक्रोशमृच्छेन्न वृथा वदेच्च
न पैशुनं जनवादं च कुर्यात् ।
सत्यव्रतो मितभाषोऽप्रमत्तः
तथास्य वाग्द्वारमथो सुगुप्तम् ॥ 12.269.25

nakrosamricchenna vritha vadecca
na paisunam janavadam ca kuryat
satyavrato mitabhasopramattah
tathasya vagdvaramatho suguptam

—12.269.25

Simple meaning—Vocal skill includes *(i)* polite speech, *(ii)* speaking what is relevant, *(iii)* speech that is free from ill will, *(iv)* truthful speech and *(v)* speech that uses carefully chosen words. The Mahabharata says in Vana Parva that Savitri's speech, addressed to the God of Death, had all these qualities, and because of that, Yama (God of Death) made her 'calamity - free'. Savitri's story is summarized in Chapter Eight of this book.

2.15 Skill in action कर्मकौशल (karmakausala)

Shanti Parva uses the expressions 'karmakausala' and 'daksya' interchangeably.

Apad-dharma says that skill in action is particularly important if all efforts to avert conflict fail, and calamity is caused by armed aggression. Illustrative material (or historical narration) in support of this statement is available from Virata Parva (*i.e.* Parva No. 4). Matsya Kingdom faced aggression on two fronts simultaneously, because Duryodhana and Susharma hatched a plot. However, skilful action by Arjuna and Bhima thwarted aggression on both the fronts and helped Matsya Kingdom preserve its independence and peaceful existence. Details regarding this protective action of the Pandavas are given in Chapter Twelve of this book, but a one-shloka summary is given here.

मत्स्यराज्यस्य सामर्थ्यमपर्याप्तं रक्षणार्थम् ।
पाण्डवानां बलं प्राप्य त्वापद्मुक्तिः सुलभा हि ॥ 4.72.22

matsyarajyasya samarthyamaparyaptam raksanartham
pandavanam balam prapya tvapadmuktih sulabha hi
—4.72.22

Simple meaning—Matsya Kingdom, by itself, was not strong enough to protect itself. However, with the support of the Pandavas, the Matsyas became strong enough to face two calamities successfully.

2.16 Apad-dharma says that the greatness of the Pandavas' action should be assessed from two considerations.

दाक्ष्येण कुर्वतो कर्म निष्कृत्या प्रतितिष्ठति । 12.139.88

daksyena kurvato karma niskritya pratitisthati
—12.139.88

Simple meaning—Skill in action is only one aspect of the help given by the Pandavas. The second aspect is that they gave this help in the spirit of 'mutual support' (*i.e.* treating help received as a debt, which is repaid by offering help in return).

In fact, Virata Parva explains how Yudhisthira emphasized the second aspect.

उषिताः स्म सुखं सर्वे सर्वकामैः सुपूजिताः ।
भीमसेन त्वया कार्या तस्य वासस्य निष्कृतिः ॥ 4.33.13

usitah sma sukham sarve sarvakamaih supujitah
bhimasena tvaya karya tasya vasasya niskritih
—4.33.13

Simple meaning—Yudhisthira said, "My dear Bhima, you know how grateful we are to King Virata - he has given us shelter and we have spent one year comfortably, in disguise. Now is the time for us to do some thing in return."

2.17 Shanti Parva has generalized this concept in terms of 'mutual indebtedness'.

ऋणवन्तः सदा मर्त्याः । 12.269.16
तस्मादनृणतां व्रजेत् । 12.292.9
rinavantah sada martyah

—12.269.16

tasmadanrinatam vrajet

—12.292.9

Simple meaning—Human beings should recognize that they are always indebted to society (for having brought them up and for having developed their capability). To apply their capability and work for doing good to the society, is the right way to repay their debt.

The philosophical expression for this approach is 'lokasamgraha' (good of all). And Mahabharata's philosophy can be characterized by the assertion that Karmayoga is like a coin, one side of which is skill in action, and the other side is lokasamgraha (good of all). Therefore, skill in action and lokasamgraha go together.

2.18 In view of the above, we want to refer here to a Mahabharata narration that illustrates what form lokasmagraha takes in practice. Mahaprasthanika Parva (*i.e.* Parva No. 17) describes how Yudhisthira, believing in the philosophy of lokasamgraha (good of all), refused to enter heaven "alone". Details relating to this are given in Chapter Eleven of this book, but the main shloka of that narration is given here.

तस्मान्नाहं जातु कथंचनाद्य
त्यक्ष्याम्येनं स्वसुखार्थी महेन्द्र ॥ 17.3.11
tasmannaham jatu kathancanadya
tyaksyamyenam svasukharthi mahendra

—17.3.11

Simple meaning—Yudhisthira said to Indra, "My final decision is that, for the sake of my own happiness, I shall not abandon this dog today, under any circumstances."

2.19 Change of priorities प्राथमिकता परिवर्तन (prathamikata parivartana)

Shanti Parva says that the traditional Varnashrama-dharma is meant for times of peace, but needs to be adjusted for times of crisis.

अन्यो धर्मः समस्थस्य विषमस्थस्य चापरः ।
आपदस्तु कथं शक्याः परिपाठेन वेदितुम् ॥ 12.260.4

anyo dharmah samasthasya visamasthasya caparah
apadastu katham sakyah paripathena veditum
—12.260.4

Simple meaning—Duties of citizens vary, depending on whether they are living in times of peace or in times of crisis. Written texts mostly advise about times of peace (recommending varnashrama-dharma). However, if necessary adjustment is not made therein, it proves to be inappropriate to meet the challenges of a crisis.

2.20 Similarly, the traditional recommendation about having four goals of life (artha, kama, dharma, moksa) needs to be modified, because all the citizens of the state must give priority to facing the calamity successfully (which becomes the single goal of life in times of crisis).

आपद्काले राष्ट्ररक्षा ह्येक एव पुरुषार्थः । 12.165.33
ब्राह्मणो यदि वा वैश्यः शूद्रो वा राजसत्तम ॥
उत्साहेन प्रजा रक्षेद् दंडं धर्मेण धारयन् ॥
संघातधर्ममाचरेद् वर्णधर्माद् भिन्नमपि ॥ 12.78.36

apadkale rastraraksa hyeka eva purusarthah —2.165.33
brahmano yadi va vaisyah sudro va rajasattama
utsahena praja raksed dandam dharmena dharayan
sanghatadharmamacared varnadharmad bhinnamapi
—12.78.36

Simple meaning—When a state faces aggression, there is only one goal of life, viz. protection of the state, for all its citizens. Then the responsibility of protecting the state does not remain confined to ksatriyas only. All others, viz. brahmins, vaisyas and sudras, too, have to offer, and be prepared, to perform war-related functions, enthusiastically. In this way, Apad-dharma has priority over Varna-dharma, in times of crisis.

2.21 Apad-dharma gives a warning that any citizen not cooperating in the task of protecting the state, should be declared a traitor.

ये च राष्ट्रोपरोधेन वृद्धिं कुर्वन्ति केचन।
तदैव तेऽनुमार्यन्ते त्वधर्मपालका यथा॥ 12.135.21

ye ca rastroparodhena vriddhim kurvanti kecana
tadaiva tenumaryante tvadharmapalaka yatha
—12.135.21

Simple meaning—Any citizen, trying to gain personal benefit, at the cost of harming the state, is a sinner.

अकस्मात् क्रोधमोहाभ्यां लोभाद् वापि स्वभावजात्।
अन्योन्यं नाभिभाषन्ते तत्पराभवलक्षणम्॥ 12.107.29

akasmat krodhamohabhyam lobhad vapi svabhavajat
anyonyam nabhibhasante tatparabhavalaksanam
—12.107.29

Simple meaning—In order to face the crisis successfully, the state requires perfect unity among all the citizens. The key to resolve internal conflicts is purposeful dialogue, avoiding anger, obstinacy and greed. Unless all the citizens do this, willingly and gladly, and in a coordinated manner, the state will face destruction.

2.22 Shanti Parva contains a warning that, due to their internal conflicts, Yadava's are heading towards self-destruction. And this is what actually happened thirty six years later, as narrated in Mausala Parva (*i.e.* Parva No. 16). Details are given in Chapter Six of this book.

2.23 Steadfastness धृति (dhriti)

Apad-dharma says that facing a serious calamity must be viewed as a long-term effort. In such a prolonged process, there is bound to be need to make adjustments, to comply with the 'desh-kala-patra' doctrine which recommends a dynamic approach.[2] Therefore, steadfastness, and willingness to make adjustments, go together.

धृतिर्दाक्ष्यं संयमो ज्ञानवृद्धिः
धैर्यं शौर्यं देशकालाप्रमादः ।
अल्पस्य वा बहुनो वा विवृद्धौ
अर्थस्यैतानि तु समिन्धनानि ॥ 12.120.37

dhritirdaksyam samyamo jnanavriddhih
dhairyam sauryam desakalapramadah
alpasya va bahuno va vivriddhau
arthasyaitani tu samindhanani

—12.120.37

Simple meaning—At all stages of the struggle, in order to make steady progress towards the attainment of the objective, the Karmayogin will require *(i)* steadfastness, *(ii)* skill in action, *(iii)* co-ordination, *(iv)* updating of knowledge, *(v)* patience, *(vi)* enthusiasm, and *(vii)* willingness to make adjustments according to changes in time, place and circumstances, so as not to become obsolete and ineffective.

2.24 Some of the above-mentioned virtues are already referred to in the preceding paras, for example, skill in action (paras 2.15 - 2.18), coordination (para 2.7) and enthusiasm (para 2.20). Among others, emphasis on 'updating of knowledge' means that eduction and training have an important role in facing calamities. Technological improvements are also included in 'updating of knowledge'. Details regarding these are given in Chapter Seven of this book. Similarly, the importance of patience is brought out in Gautami's story (Chapter Three) and Yudhisthira's encounter with Yaksa (Chapter Nine).

2.25 Finally, the fact that Apad-dharma attaches great importance to 'willingness to make adjustments' makes Shanti Parva a revolutionary document. This encourages continuous research on the role of dharma in world peace promotion which has special significance in the 21st century.

Chapter 3

Story of Gautami's Reformist Approach towards the Killer of Her Son

3.1 The story of Gautami is narrated by Bhisma to Yudhisthira in Anusasana Parva (which is a continuation of Shanti Parva). Gautami was a peace-loving woman, who was shocked to see one day that her only son had died due to snake-bite. Gautami's neighbour, Arjunaka, out of sympathy with her, caught hold of that snake and asked Gautami to authorize the killing of that snake (to take revenge for her son's death). Then a long discussion took place between Arjunaka and Gautami, the former arguing that the snake should be killed, while the latter suggesting that the snake should be reformed and advised not to bite any child in the future. After presenting the story, we shall interpret it so as to get a message on the role of education for world peace.

3.2 गौतमी नाम कौन्तेय स्थविरा शमसंयुता ।
सर्पेण दष्टं स्वं पुत्रमपश्यद्गतचेतनम् ॥ 13.1.17

gautami nama kaunteya sthavira samasamyuta
sarpena dastam svam putramapasyadgatacetanam
—13.1.17

Simple meaning—Gautami, the mother of a son, wanted to live in peace, but one day she was shocked to see that her only son had died due to snake-bite.

अथ तं स्नायुपाशेन बद्ध्वा सर्पममर्षितः ।
लुब्धकोऽर्जुनको नाम गौतम्याः समुपानयत् ॥ 13.1.18

atha tam snayupasena baddhva sarpamamarsitah
lubdhakorjunako nama gautamyah samupanayat
—13.1.18

Simple meaning—Gautami's neighbour, Arjunaka, out of sympathy with her, caught hold of that snake and came to her (with a view to obtaining her approval for killing that snake, to take revenge for the son's death).

स चाब्रवीदयं ते स पुत्रहा पन्नगाधमः ।
ब्रूहि क्षिप्रं महाभागे वध्यतां केन हेतुना ॥ 13.1.19
sa cabravidayam te sa putraha pannagadhamah
bruhi ksipram mahabhage vadhyatam kena hetuna
—13.1.19

Simple meaning—Arjunaka sympathized with Gautami, saying, "O great lady, I am so sorry that your son has died, but I have caught hold of the snake who killed your son. Please authorize me to kill the snake, to take revenge for the son's death."

अग्नौ प्रक्षिप्यतामेष च्छिद्यतां खण्डशोऽपि वा ।
न ह्ययं बालहा पापश्चिरं जीवितुमर्हति ॥ 13.1.20
agnau praksipyatamesa cchidyatam khandasopi va
na hyayam balaha papasciram jivitumarhati
—13.1.20

Simple meaning—Arjunaka asked Gautami, "Shall I throw the snake into fire or shall I hack it into pieces? Since it has committed the sin of killing your son, it must receive the appropriate punishment, viz. get killed, one way or the other."

3.3 गौतम्युवाच
विसृजैनमबुद्धिस्त्वमवध्योऽर्जुनक त्वया ।
को ह्यात्मानं गुरुं कुर्यात् प्राप्तव्यमविचिन्तयन् ॥ 13.1.21
gautamyuvaca
visrijainamabuddhistvamavadhyorjunaka tvaya
ko hyatmanam gurum kuryat praptavyamavicintayan
—13.1.21

Simple meaning—Gautami's reply came as a big surprise to Arjunaka, because she said, "My dear Arjunaka, please reconsider and take back the words that you spoke to me. Obviously, your understanding is not right. You say that the snake committed the sin by killing my son, but will you too not commit the sin if you kill the snake?"

प्लवन्ते धर्मलघवो लोकेऽम्भसि यथा प्लवा: ।
मज्जन्ति पापगुरव: शस्त्रं स्कन्नमिवोदके ॥ 13.1.22
plavante dharmalaghavo lokembhasi yatha plavah
majjanti papaguravah sastram skannamivodake
—13.1.22

Simple meaning—Gautami, explaining her initial remark, said, "My dear, since killing is a sin, it follows that not only the initial killer but also the one who kills in revenge - both are sinners. Furthermore, all killers, because of the burden that automatically arises from the sin that they commit, drown into the ocean of samsara". Obviously, Gautami is quoting from scriptures which depict life symbolically, as a voyage by sea—righteous people easily cross the sea *i.e.* lead a happy life, but sinners get drowned *i.e.* lead a miserable life.

हत्वा चैनं नामृत: स्यादयं मे
जीवत्यस्मिन् कोऽत्यय: स्यादयं ते ।
अस्योत्सर्गे प्राणयुक्तस्य जन्तो:
मृत्योर्लोकं को नु गच्छेदनन्तम् ॥ 13.1.23
hatva cainam namritah syadayam me
jivatyasmin kotyayah syadayam te
asyotsarge pranayuktasya jantoh
mrityorlokam ko nu gacchedanantam
—13.1.23

Simple meaning—Gautami concluded, "My dear Arjunaka, thank you for your desire and effort to help me, but please tell me: Will my son become alive again when you kill this snake? Obviously "no". Therefore I am not in favour of killing the snake. Furthermore, if the snake is not killed, will that cause any harm to you? Again, why would you like to expose yourself to Yama's punishment by committing the sin of killing?" As earlier, Gautami quotes from scriptures which depict Yama symbolically as the impartial judge who punishes all killers.

3.4 अर्जुनक उवाच
जानाम्यहं देवि गुणागुणज्ञे
सर्वार्तियुक्ता गुरवो भवन्ति ।
स्वस्थस्यैते तूपदेशा भवन्ति
तस्मात् क्षुद्रं सर्पमेनं हनिष्ये ॥ 13.1.24

arjunaka uvaca
janamyaham devi gunagunajne
sarvartiyukta guravo bhavanti
svasthasyaite tupadesa bhavanti
tasmat ksudram sarpamenam hanisye

—13.1.24

Simple meaning—Arjunaka again argued that the snake should be killed, "O great lady, your knowledge of scriptures is unique, and you have a very kind heart, therefore you do not want to harm the snake, inspite of the fact that it killed your son. But in my opinion, you should not apply your benevolent philosophy to the present situation, because the snake does not deserve kindness."

शमार्थिनः कालगतिं वदन्ति
सद्यः शुचं त्वर्थविदस्त्यजन्ति ।
श्रेयःक्षयं शोचति नित्यमोहात्
तस्माच्छुचं मुञ्च हते भुजंगे ॥ 13.1.25

samarthinah kalagatim vadanti
sadyah sucam tvarthavidastyajanti
sreyahksayam socati nityamohat
tasmacchucam munca hate bhujange

—13.1.25

Simple meaning—Next, Arjunaka pleaded for the killing of the snake from another perspective, "O great lady, there are three ways of handling a crisis situation. Peace-loving people like you take the view that, instead of blaming the snake, the person who ordered the snake to kill your son, should be blamed. This is the first of the three ways of handling the crisis, and is a philosophic approach. The second way is that of worldly people—they punish the killer (*i.e.* the snake) and then feel relieved. I belong to this category, and I feel that you should allow me to kill the snake, at least for my sake. The third way is that of self-torturing people—they take no steps to tide over the crisis and therefore allow the pain to remain in their heart for the rest of their life. I am glad that neither you nor I belong to this category."

3.5 गौतम्युवाच
आर्तिर्नैवं विद्यतेऽस्मद्विधानां
धर्मात्मानः सर्वदा सज्जना हि ।
नित्यायस्तो बालकोऽप्यस्य तस्माद्
ईशे नाहं पन्नगस्य प्रमाथे ॥ 13.1.26

gautamyuvaca
artirnaivam vidyatesmadvidhanam
dharmatmanah sarvada sajjana hi
nityayasto balakopyasya tasmad
ise naham pannagasya pramathe

—13.1.26

Simple meaning—Gautami replied to Arjunaka's plea based on three categories, "My dear Arjunaka, the three categories that you have mentioned refer to three kinds of people, and our scriptures call them sattvika, rajasi and tamasika. You have correctly put me in the first category. My first priority is peace, which cannot be disturbed, even by the death of my son. I don't consider the snake to be responsible for my son's death (may be the snake was only the visible cause). Therefore I am unable to authorize the killing of the snake".

न सात्त्विकानां कोपोऽस्ति कुतः कोपाच्च यातनाम् ।
मार्दवान् क्षम्यतां साधो मुच्यतामेष पन्नगः ॥ 13.1.27

na sattvikanam koposti kutah kopacca yatanam
mardavan ksamyatam sadho mucyatamesa pannagah
—13.1.27

Simple meaning—Gautami pleaded for compassion towards the snake, "My dear, sattvika people are free from anger, violence, and desire for revenge, and I suggest that you too be kind and forgiving, and release this snake out of compassion".

3.6 अर्जुनक उवाच
हत्वा लाभः श्रेय एवाव्ययः स्यात्
लभ्यो लाभः स्याद् बलिभ्यः प्रशस्तः ।
कालाल्लाभो यस्तु सत्यो भवेत
श्रेयो लाभः कुत्सितेऽस्मिन्न ते स्यात् ॥ 13.1.28

arjunaka uvaca
hatva labhah sreya evavyayah syat
labhyo labhah syad balibhyah prasastah
kalallabho yastu satyo bhaveta
sreyo labhah kutsitesminna te syat
—13.1.28

Simple meaning—Arjunaka argued that keeping dangerous people alive cannot benefit anyone, "O great lady, to be free from anger is not always good, because dangerous people, if kept alive, can harm so many persons. Therefore, in my opinion, dangerous people should be killed, not forgiven, after their killing habit has come to light".

3.7 गौतम्युवाच
का नु प्राप्तिर्गृह्य शत्रुं निहत्य
का कामाप्तिः प्राप्य शत्रुं न मुक्त्वा ।
कस्मात् सौम्याहं न क्षमे नो भुजंगे
मोक्षार्थं वा कस्य हेतोर्न कुर्याम् ॥ 13.1.29

gautamyuvaca
ka nu praptirgrihya satrum nihatya
ka kamaptih prapya satrum na muktva

kasmat saumyaham na ksame no bhujange
moksartham va kasya hetorna kuryam

—13.1.29

Simple meaning—The exchange of conflicting arguments between Gautami and Arjunaka continued. While Arjunaka put forward the worldly people's point of view, Gautami put forward the viewpoint of peace-loving people, "My dear Arjunaka, I am not in favour of capturing the killer and then putting him to death. Governments have a process for punishing the culprits, but they too have a provision for listening to arguments for their release".

3.8 अर्जुनक उवाच
अस्मादेकाद् बहवो रक्षितव्या
नैको बहुभ्यो गौतमि रक्षितव्यः ।
कृतागसं धर्मविदस्त्यजन्ति
सरीसृपं पापमिमं जहि त्वं ॥ 13.1.30
arjunaka uvaca
asmadekad bahavo raksitavya
naiko bahubhyo gautami raksitavyah
kritagasam dharmavidastyajanti
sarisripam papamimam jahi tvam

—13.1.30

Simple meaning—Arjunaka argued why punishment is better than forgiveness, "O great lady, please keep in mind that this snake, if forgiven, might kill several more children. Therefore, by protecting one snake, you might indirectly increase the risk to several children. Our dharma cannot justify such an approach. If you reconsider the views of the scriptures from this angle, then you will authorize me to kill this snake".

3.9 गौतम्युवाच
नास्मिन् हते पन्नगे पुत्रको मे
सम्प्राप्स्यते लुब्धक जीवितं वै ।
गुणं चान्यं नास्य वधे प्रपश्ये
तस्मात् सर्पं लुब्धक मुंच जीवन् ॥ 13.1.31

gautamyuvaca
nasmin hate pannage putrako me
samprapsyate lubdhaka jivitam vai
gunam canyam nasya vadhe prapasye
tasmat sarpam lubdhaka munca jivan
—13.1.31

Simple meaning—Although Gautami had a lot of patience, yet she did not want to prolong the exchange of arguments, therefore she concluded, "My dear Arjunaka, at this time, I give priority to only one consideration viz. whether by killing this snake, you can bring my son back to life. Obviously 'not'. The other consideration whether this snake, if kept alive, might kill other children, may appeal to Governments, but not to me. Therefore, I cannot authorize you to kill this snake, who was probably ordered by someone else to kill my son".

3.10 As soon as Gautami referred to "someone else", the snake spoke up and addressed Arjunaka -

को न्वर्जुनक दोषोऽत्र विद्यते मम बालिश ।
अस्वतंत्रं हि मां मृत्युर्विवशं यदचूचुदत् ॥ 13.1.35
तस्यायं वचनाद् दष्टो न कोपेन न काम्यया ।
वधमथवा शिक्षणं तत्कुरुष्व मृत्युं प्रति ॥ 13.1.36

ko nvarjunaka dosotra vidyate mama balisa
asvatantram hi mam mrityurvivasam yadacucudat
—13.1.35

tasyayam vacanad dasto na kopena na kamyaya
vadhamathava siksanam tatkurusva mrityum prati
—13.1.36

Simple meaning—The snake said, "Dear Arjunaka, you do not know all the facts, and are therefore blaming me for the death of the boy. The fact is that I am just a tool. The plan for killing the boy was drawn up by Mrityu who used me as a tool. Personally, I had no quarrel with the boy. So Mrityu is to be blamed, not me, and whether you want to kill the culprit or educate the culprit, all that should be directed to Mrityu, not to me".

3.11 Anusasana Parva's story does not end here. However, the above-mentioned part of the story is enough to give us three messages:-

(i) Following Gautami's example, the victim's mother need not take the law into her own hands.

(ii) It is for the Government to decide what to do to the killer, but Gautami's preference was for "Reform, not revenge".

(iii) Educational programs for promoting friendliness should cover not only the school-going children but also adults who are exploiting these children for their anti-social (terroristic)activities.[1]

CHAPTER 4

Story of a Non-violent Scholar Who Won Over a Violent Monster

4.1 The story narrated in this chapter glorifies the non-violent way of bringing about a change of heart, and is narrated by Bhisma to Yudhisthira in Anusasana Parva (like the story in the preceding chapter). A non-violent scholar was captured by a violent monster but instead of fighting back or helplessly yielding to be killed, the scholar entered into a dialogue with his captor. The monster was impressed by the scholar's sweet words and calm face, and so he said, "I shall release you if you give me a satisfactory reply to my question: Why am I pale and lean?" At the end of their dialogue, the monster's heart was converted, and he adopted a peace-loving frame of mind, becomig a friend of the scholar. Such stories occurring in Buddhist literature are well-known, but this story does not seem to have attracted much attention, partly because the scholar's name is not specified in the Mahabharata.

4.2 भीष्म उवाच

कश्चिद् वाग्बुद्धिसम्पन्नो ब्राह्मणो विजने वने।
गृहीतः कृच्छ्रमापन्नो रक्षसा भक्षयिष्यता ॥ 13.124.5

kascid vagbuddhisampanno brahmano vijane vane
grihitah kricchramapanno raksasa bhaksayisyata
—13.124.5

Simple meaning—A certain scholar, endowed with vocal skill as well as intelligence, fell into distress, because he was seized in a lone forest by a monster who wanted to eat him up.

स बुद्धिश्रुतिसम्पन्नस्तं दृष्ट्वातीव भीषणम् ।
सामैवास्मिन् प्रयुयुजे न मुमोह न विव्यथे ॥ 13.124.6

sa buddhisrutisampannastam dristvativa bhisanam
samaivasmin prayuyuje na mumoha na vivyathe
—13.124.6

Simple meaning—Since the scholar was well-versed in scriptures, he kept his calm. Without allowing himself to be stupefied at the sight of that terrible cannibal, he resolved to apply the method of non-violence.

4.3 रक्षस्तु वाचं सम्पूज्य प्रश्नं पप्रच्छ तं द्विजम् ।
मोक्ष्यसे ब्रूहि मे प्रश्नं केनास्मि हरिणः कृशः ॥ 13.124.7

raksastu vacam sampujya prasnam papraccha tam dvijam
moksyase bruhi me prasnam kenasmi harinah krisah
—13.124.7

Simple meaning—The monster was impressed by the scholar's sweet words and calm face. He did not carry out his initial intention of killing the scholar. Rather he offered to give him a chance by saying. "I shall release you if you give me a satisfactory reply to my question: Why am I pale and lean".

मुहूर्तमथ संचिन्त्य ब्राह्मणस्तस्य रक्षसः ।
आभिर्गाथाभिरव्यग्रः प्रश्नं प्रतिजगाद ह ॥ 13.124.8

muhurtamatha sancintya brahmanastasya raksasah
abirgathabhiravyagrah prasnam pratijagada ha
—13.124.8

Simple meaning—After reflecting for a while, the scholar calmly accepted the conditional offer of the monster and proceeded to give his reply in the following well-spoken words.

4.4 ब्राह्मण उवाच
विदेशस्थो विलोकस्थो विना नूनं सुहृज्जनैः ।
विषयानतुलान् भुङ्क्षे तेनासि हरिणः कृशः ॥ 13.124.9

brahmana uvaca
videsastho vilokastho vina nunam suhrijjanaih
visayanatulan bhunkse tenasi harinah krisah

—13.124.9

Simple meaning—The scholar said to the monster, "Dwelling in a place that is distant from your normal abode, moving in a different environment, and deprived of the companionship of your friends and kinsmen, you find yourself in possession of unusual sense objects. Such a situation makes you pale and lean".

नूनं मित्राणि ते रक्षः साधूपचरितान्यपि ।
स्वदोषादपरज्यन्ते तेनासि हरिणः कृशः ॥ 13.124.10
nunam mitrani te raksah sadhupacaritanyapi
svadosadaparajyante tenasi harinah krisah

—13.124.10

Simple meaning—"Your friends, though well-treated by you, are still not well-disposed towards you—and this is not due to your fault, but because of their own vicious nature. That makes you pale and lean".

4.5 धनैश्वर्याधिकाः स्तब्धास्त्वद्गुणैः परमावराः ।
अवजानन्ति नूनं त्वां तेनासि हरिणः कृशः ॥ 13.124.11
dhanaisvaryadhikah stabdhastvadgunaih paramavarah
avajananti nunam tvam tenasi harinah krisah

—13.124.11

Simple meaning—"Persons less qualified than you, happen to get greater wealth and prosperity than you. When they look down upon you, then you become pale and lean".

गुणवान् विगुणानन्यान् नूनं पश्यसि सत्कृतान् ।
प्राज्ञोऽप्राज्ञान् विनीतात्मा तेनासि हरिणः कृशः ॥ 13.124.12
gunavan vigunananyan nunam pasyasi satkritan
prajnoprajnan vinitatma tenasi harinah krisah

—13.124.12

Simple meaning—"Inspite of deserving honour due to your qualities, wisdom and modesty, you do not get it, while you see that honour bestowed on those who have no qualities and no wisdom—this makes you pale and lean".

4.6 अवृत्त्या क्लिश्यमानोऽपि वृत्त्युपायान् विगर्हयन् ।
माहात्म्याद् व्यथसे नूनं तेनासि हरिणः कृशः ॥ 13.124.13
avrittya klisyamanopi vrittyupayan vigarhayan
mahatmyad vyathase nunam tenasi harinah krisah
—13.124.13

Simple meaning—"Though distressed through want of means of support, you are led by the greatness of your soul to disregard unworthy means (like living on charity). This dilemma makes you pale and lean".

4.7 सम्पीड्यात्मानमार्यत्वात् त्वया कश्चिदुपस्कृतः ।
जितं त्वां मन्यते साधो तेनासि हरिणः कृशः ॥ 13.124.14
sampidyatmanamaryatvat tvaya kascidupaskritah
jitam tvam manyate sadho tenasi harinah krisah
—13.124.14

Simple meaning—"Even when you do good to someone (and this might involve sacrifice on your part but you still do it because of your good nature), that person (instead of appreciating your help) thinks that your action is only a sign of your weakness. Such an unpleasant experience makes you pale and lean".

4.8 क्लिश्यमानान् विमार्गेषु कामक्रोधावृतात्मनः ।
मन्ये त्वं ध्यायसि जनांस्तेनासि हरिणः कृशः ॥ 13.124.15
klisyamanan vimargesu kamakrodhavritatmanah
manye tvam dhyayasi janamstenasi harinah krisah
—13.124.15

Simple meaning—"Perhaps you feel sorry for those persons who follow a wrong path under the influence of lust and anger, and who therefore suffer misery in this world. Such sympathy for sinners makes you pale and lean".

4.9 प्रज्ञासंभावितो नूनमप्रज्ञैरुपसंहितः ।
हीयमानोऽसि दुर्वृत्तैस्तेनासि हरिणः कृशः ॥ 13.124.16

prajnasambhavito nunamprajnairupasamhitah
hiyamanosi durvrittaistenasi harinah krisah

—13.124.16

Simple meaning—"Even though you deserve honour due to your wisdom, you find that unwise persons laugh at you and wicked persons insult you. To be a victim of such baseless illtreatment makes you pale and lean".

नूनं मित्रमुखः शत्रुः कश्चिदार्यवदाचरन् ।
वञ्चयित्वा गतस्त्वां वै तेनासि हरिणः कृशः ॥ 13.124.17
nunam mitramukhah satruh kascidaryavadacaran
vancayitva gatastvam vai tenasi harinah krisah

—13.124.17

Simple meaning—"Perhaps some enemy of yours pretended to be friendly with you, spoke sweet words and behaved nicely, but subsequently cheated you and went away. To be a victim of such hypocrisy and cheating makes you pale and lean".

4.10 प्रकाशार्थगतिर्नूनं रहस्यकुशलः कृती ।
तज्ज्ञैर्न पूज्यसे नूनं तेनासि हरिणः कृशः ॥ 13.124.18
prakasarthagatirnunam rahasyakusalah kriti
tajjnairna pujyase nunam tenasi harinah krisah

—13.124.18

Simple meaning—"Even those people do not respect you who know about your learning, your skill in understanding different issues and your efficient method of work. Such non-recognition of your talent makes you pale and lean".

असत्स्वपि निविष्टेषु ब्रुवतो मुक्तसंशयम् ।
गुणास्ते न विराजन्ते तेनासि हरिणः कृशः ॥ 13.124.19
asatsvapi nivistesu bruvato muktasamsayam
gunaste na virajante tenasi harinah krisah

—13.124.19

Simple meaning—"Even though you speak clearly and remove the confusion from which wicked and untruthful persons suffer, you do not get due credit for the fine contribution that you make. Such non-recognition of your qualities makes you pale and lean".

4.11 धनबुद्धिश्रुतैर्हीनः केवलं तेजसान्वितः ।
महत् प्रार्थयसे नूनं तेनासि हरिणः कृशः ॥ 13.124.20
dhanabuddhisrutairhinah kevalam tejasanvitah
mahat prarthayase nunam tenasi harinah krisah
—13.124.20

Simple meaning—"Perhaps you wanted a high position, merely on the basis of your physical strength, and you were unsuccessful because you did not have the necessary wealth, intelligence and scriptural knowledge. Such failure makes you pale and lean".

4.12 तपःप्रणिहितात्मानं मन्ये त्वारण्यकांक्षिणम् ।
बान्धवा नाभिनन्दन्ति तेनासि हरिणः कृशः ॥ 13.124.21
tapahpranihitatmanam manye tvaranyakanksinam
bandhava nabhinandanti tenasi harinah krisah
—13.124 .21

Simple meaning—"It seems that, although you are keen to retire into the forest to carry out your plan to practice severe austerities, yet your kinsmen are not favourably inclined towards this plan of yours. Such non-cooperation from your kinsmen makes you pale and lean".

4.13 इष्टभार्यस्य ये नूनं प्रातिवेश्यो महाधनः ।
युवा सुललितः कामी तेनासि हरिणः कृशः ॥ 13.124.22
istabharyasya ye nunam prativesyo mahadhanah
yuva sulalitah kami tenasi harinah krisah
—13.124.22

Simple meaning—"While living in the city, you may notice that, some neighbour of yours, who is rich, young and handsome, is trying to attract the attention of your dear wife. Such threat from your neighbour makes you pale and lean".

नूनमर्थवतां मध्ये तव वाक्यमनुत्तमम् ।
न भाति कालेऽभिहितं तेनासि हरिणः कृशः ॥ 13.124.23

nunamarthavatam madhye tava vakyamanuttamam
na bhati kalebhihitam tenasi harinah krisah

—13.124.23

Simple meaning—"While in the company of rich persons, you may find that, howsoever wisely you speak, they criticize your words as being unwise and inappropriate to the occasion. Such criticism make you pale and lean".

दृढपूर्वं श्रुतं मूर्खं कुपितं हृदयप्रियम् ।
अनुनेतुं न शक्नोषि तेनासि हरिण: कृश: ॥ 13.124.24
dridhapurvam srutam murkham kupitam hridayapriyam
anunetum na saknosi tenasi harinah krisah

—13.124.24

Simple meaning—"While in the company of your dear kinsmen, you may find that one of them, though exposed to scriptures for a long time, acts foolishly and becomes angry with you, and you are unable to pacify him. Such inability makes you pale and lean".

4.14 नूनमासंजयित्वा त्वां कृत्ये कस्मिंश्चिदीप्सिते ।
कश्चिदर्थयते नित्यं तेनासि हरिण: कृश: ॥ 13.124.25
nunamasanjayitva tvam kritye kasmimscidipsite
kascidarthayate nityam tenasi harinah krisah

—13.124.25

Simple meaning—"While dealing with a business partner, you may find that, although outwardly he gives the impression that the work allotted to you is to fulfill your desires and your purposes, in reality he only wants to promote his own selfish interest. Such disillusionment makes you pale and lean".

नूनं त्वां सुगुणैर्युक्तं पूजयानं सुहृद्ध्रुवम् ।
ममार्थमिति जानीते तेनासि हरिण: कृश: ॥ 13.124.26
nunam tvam sugunairyuktam pujayanam suhriddhruvam
mamarthamiti janite tenasi harinah krisah

—13.124.26

Simple meaning—"While dealing with a friend, you may find that, although people known to both of you honour you for your qualities, still your friend thinks that such honour is given to you because of him. Such betrayal by a friend makes you pale and lean".

4.15 अन्तर्गतमभिप्रायं नूनं नेच्छसि लज्जया ।
विवेक्तुं प्राप्तिशैथिल्यात् तेनासि हरिणः कृशः ॥ 13.124.27

antargatamabhiprayam nunam necchasi lajjaya
vivektum praptisaithilyat tenasi harinah krisah
—13.124.27

Simple meaning—"While dealing with a potential donor, you may find that two reasons prevent you from stating clearly what you want—the first reason being that you have doubts about getting what you want, and the second reason being that you feel ashamed in exposing your weakness. Such an awareness about your own problems makes you pale and lean".

4.16 नानाबुद्धिरुचो लोके मनुष्यान् नूनमिच्छसि ।
ग्रहीतुं स्वगुणैः सर्वोस्तेनासि हरिणः कृशः ॥ 13.124.28

nanabuddhiruco loke manusyan nunamicchasi
grahitum svagunaih sarvostenasi harinah krisah
—13.124.28

Simple meaning—"You might have set before yourself an impossible goal, viz. to bring under your control, all the people who have diverse kinds of understanding and inclination. Such an over- estimation of your own capability makes you pale and lean".

अविद्वान् भीरुरल्पार्थे विद्याविक्रमदानजम् ।
यशः प्रार्थयसे नूनं तेनासि हरिणः कृशः ॥ 13.124.29

avidvan bhiruralparthe vidyavikramadanajam
yasah prarthayase nunam tenasi harinah krisah
—13.124.29

Simple meaning—"Another impossible goal that you might have set before yourself is this, viz. that you seek such fame as is won by knowledge, prowess and gifts, but you do not have learning, courage and wealth. Such an unbalanced approach on your part makes you pale and lean".

4.17 चिराभिलषितं किंचित्फलमप्राप्तमेव ते ।
कृतमन्यैरपहृतं तेनासि हरिणः कृशः ॥ 13.124.30
cirabhilasitam kincitphalamapraptameva te
kritamanyairapahritam tenasi harinah krisah

—13.124.30

Simple meaning—"You might have been trying hard to acquire some long-desired object, only to find that some other persons have taken it away, leaving you disappointed. Such a failure afer a long struggle makes you pale and lean".

नूनमात्मकृतं दोषमपश्यन् किंचिदात्मनः ।
अकारणेऽभिशप्तोऽसि तेनासि हरिणः कृशः ॥ 13.124.31
nunamatmakritam dosamapasyan kincidatmanah
akaranebhisaptosi tenasi harinah krisah

—13.124.31

Simple meaning—"The unhelpful attitude of other persons might hurt you in another way, viz. that, although you are completely innocent and are unable to detect any error on your part, but still other persons curse you, apparently for no good reason. Such a false criticism by other persons makes you pale and lean".

4.18 साधून् गृहस्थान् दृष्ट्वा तथासाधून् वनेचरान् ।
मुक्तांश्चावसथे सक्तांस्तेनासि हरिणः कृशः ॥ 13.124.32
sadhun grihasthan dristva tathasadhun vanecaran
muktamscavasathe saktanstenasi harinah krisah

—13.124.32

Simple meaning—"As a well-wisher of others, you may feel disappointed when you see strange behaviour on their part, for example, samnyasins reverting to householders' way of life, worldly persons living in forests, and liberated souls getting attached to property. Such disappointment makes you pale and lean".

सुहृदानां दुःखमार्तानां न प्रमोक्ष्यसि चार्तिजम् ।
अलमर्थगुणैर्हीनं तेनासि हरिणः कृशः ॥ 13.124.33

suhridanam duhkhamartanam na pramoksyasi cartijam
alamarthagunairhinam tenasi harinah krisah
—13.124.33

Simple meaning—"As a well-wisher of others, you may also feel unhappy that you do not have the necessary wealth and resources, to dispel the grief of your friends and the sufferings of sorrowing people. Such unhappiness makes you pale and lean".

धर्म्यमर्थ्यं च काम्यं च काले चाभिहितं वचः ।
न प्रतीयन्ति ते नूनं तेनासि हरिणः कृशः ॥ 13.124.34

dharmyamarthyam ca kamyam ca kale cabhihitam vacah
na pratiyanti te nunam tenasi harinah krisah
—13.124.34

Simple meaning—"As a well-wisher of others, you may also feel rejected when they do not trust you, although you speak well-timed words, consistent with dharma, to promote wealth and psychological values. Such rejection makes you pale and lean".

4.19 दत्तानकुशलैरर्थान् मनीषी संजिजीविषुः ।
प्राप्य वर्तयसे नूनं तेनासि हरिणः कृशः ॥ 13.124.35

dattanakusalairarthan manisi sanjijivisuh
prapya vartayase nunam tenasi harinah krisah
—13.125.35

Simple meaning—"As a believer in the law of karma, you might be afraid of evil consequences when you accept a gift from a person of evil conduct, to help you maintain yourself, particularly because you are wise enough to understand what dharma means. Such fear makes you pale and lean".

पापान् प्रवर्धतो दृष्ट्वा कल्याणानावसीदतः ।
ध्रुवं गर्हयसे नित्यं तेनासि हरिणः कृशः ॥

13.124.36

papan pravardhato dristva kalyanavasidatah
dhruvam garhayase nityam tenasi harinah krisah
—13.124.36

Simple meaning—"As a believer in the law of karma, you might be confused when you see unrighteous people advancing and righteous people suffering, although you try to promote dharma by condemning the system which violates the law of dharma. Such confusion makes you pale and lean".

4.20 परस्परविरुद्धानां प्रियं नूनं चिकीर्षसि।
सुहृदामुपरोधेन तेनासि हरिणः कृशः ॥ 13.124.37
parasparaviruddhanam priyam nunam cikirsasi
suhridamuparodhena tenasi harinah krisah
—13.124.37

Simple menaing—"Desirous of reforming your friends, who fight among themselves, you try to bring them together, for their good, but probably you are worried about the degree of success. Such worry makes you pale and lean".

श्रोत्रियांश्च विकर्मस्थान् प्राज्ञांश्चाप्यजितेन्द्रियान् ।
मन्येऽनुध्यायसि जनांस्तेनासि हरिणः कृशः ॥ 13.124.38
srotriyamsca vikarmasthan prajnamscapyajitendriyan
manyenudhyayasi janamstenasi harinah krisah
—13.124.38

Simple meaning—"Desirous of reforming important persons, you try to help, for example, you try that Vedic scholars should get away from improper acts, and other learned persons should similarly get out of the slavery of their senses, but probably you are worried about the degree of success. Such worry makes you pale and lean".

4.21 एवं सम्पूजितं रक्षो विप्रं तं प्रत्यपूजयत् ।
सखायमकरोच्चैनं संयोज्यार्थैर्मुमोच ह ॥ 13.124.39
evam sampujitam rakso vipram tam pratyapujayat
sakhayamakaroccainam samyojyarthairmumoca ha
—13.124.39

Simple meaning—Concluding the story, Bhisma said to Yudhisthira, "After getting such a fine and respectful reply to his question, the monster too adopted a worshipful attitude, viz. that he made the scholar his friend, and (instead of eating him up), gave him a nice gift of money, and let him off to freedom"[1].

CHAPTER 5

Story of a Mouse Who Protected Himself from Three Enemies

5.1 The story of a wise mouse is an important narration of Apad-dharma. The mouse had three enemies, viz. a cat, an owl, and a mongoose. After considering all options, the mouse made peace with the cat. The other two enemies then disappeared from the scene. Finally, through a brilliant use of his brain, the mouse protected himself from the cat too. Obviously, the purpose of the story is to show to human beings how they should face a calamity characterized by a multiplicity of adversaries. Apad-dharma's message is : If a mouse can protect himself, why can't human beings achieve similar success?

5.2 वने महति कस्मिंश्चिन्न्यग्रोधः सुमहानभूत् ।
लताजालपरिच्छिन्नो नानाद्विजगणान्वितः ॥ 12. 138.19

vane mahati kasmimscinnyagrodhah sumahanabhut
latajalaparicchinno nanadvijagananvitah
—12.138.19

Simple meaning—There was a large banyan tree in the midst of an extensive forest. Covered with many kinds of creepers, this tree was the resort of diverse species of birds.

तस्य मूलं समाश्रित्य कृत्वा शतमुखं बिलम् ।
वसतिस्म महाप्राज्ञः पलितो नाम मूषिकः ॥ 12. 138.21

tasya mulam samasritya kritva satamukham bilam
vasatisma mahaprajnah palito nama musikah
—12.138.21

Simple meaning—A mouse of great wisdom, named Palita, lived at the root of that tree, having made a hole there with a hundred outlets.

शाखां तस्य समाश्रित्य वसति स्म सुखं पुरा।
लोमशो नाम मार्जारः पक्षिसंघातखादकः ॥ 12.138.22

sakham tasya samasritya vasatisma sukham pura
lomaso nama marjarah paksisanghatakhadakah
—12.138.22

Simple meaning—A cat, named Lomasa, lived happily on the branches of that tree, daily devouring a large number of birds.

तत्र चागत्य चाण्डालो ह्यरन्ये कृतकेतनः।
प्रयोजयति चोन्माथं नित्यमस्तंगते रवौ ॥ 12.138.23

तत्र स्नायुमयान् पाशान् यथावत् संविधाय सः।
गृहं गत्वा सुखं शेते प्रभातामेति शर्वरीम् ॥ 12.138.24

tatra cagatya candalo hyaranye kritaketanah
prayojayati conmatham nityamastangate ravau
—12.138.23

tatra snayumayan pasan yathavat samvidhaya sah
griham gatva sukham sete prabhatameti sarvarim
—12.138.24

Simple meaning—A hunter was attracted to that spot, and he built his hut there. Every evening after sunset, he spread his net made of leather strings. Then he would happily pass the night in sleep, only to return to the spot at the dawn.

तत्र स्म नित्यं बध्यन्ते नक्तं बहुविधा मृगाः ।
कदाचिदत्र मार्जारस्त्वप्रमत्तो व्यबध्यतः ॥ 12.138.25

tatra sma nityam badhyante naktam bahuvidha mrigah
kadacidatra marjarastvapramatto vyabadhyatah
—12.138.25

Simple meaning—Diverse kinds of animals fell into the hunter's net every night. Our present story begins when one evening, Lomasa, the cat, in a moment of heedlessness, was caught in that net.

5.3 तस्मिन् बद्धे महाप्राणे शत्रौ नित्याततायिनि।
तं कालं पलितो ज्ञात्वा प्रचचार सुनिर्भयः ॥ 12.138.26

tasmin baddhe mahaprane satrau nityatatayini
tam kalam palito jnatva pracacara sunirbhayah
—12.138.26

Simple meaning—Palita, the mouse, felt at that time that since his perpetual enemy (cat) was caught in the hunter's net, he (mouse) could rove about fearlessly.

तेनानुचरता तस्मिन् वने विश्वस्तचारिणा ।
भक्ष्यं मृगयमाणेन चिराद् दृष्टं तदामिषम् ॥ 12.138.27
स तमुन्माथमारुह्य तदामिषमभक्षयत् ।
आमिषे तु प्रसक्तः स कदाचिदवलोकयन् ॥ 12.138.29

tenanucarata tasmin vane visvastacarina
bhaksyam mrigayamanena cirad dristam tadamisam
—12.138.27

sa tamunmathamaruhya tadamisamabhaksayat
amise tu prasaktah sa kadacidavalokayan
—12.138.29

Simple meaning—While roving through the forest in search of food, the mouse saw the meat which the hunter had spread there as bait. Getting upon the net, the mouse began to eat that meat, feeling free from fear. However, he suddenly noticed that there was another enemy there (*i.e.* other than the cat).

नकुलं हरिणं नाम चपलं ताम्रलोचनम् ।
तेन मूषिकगन्धेन त्वरमाणमुपागतम् ॥ 12.138.31

nakulam harinam nama capalam tamralocanam
tena musikagandhena tvaramanamupagatam
—12.138.31

Simple meaning—That enemy was a mongoose, whose name was Harina, and who was allured to that spot by the scent of the mouse.

शाखागतमरिं चान्यमपश्यत् कोटरालयम्।
उलूकं चन्द्रकं नाम तीक्ष्णतुण्डं क्षपाचरम् ॥ 12.138.32
sakhagatamarim canyamapasyat kotaralayam
ulukam candrakam nama tiksnatundam ksapacaram
—12.138.32

Simple meaning—The mouse noticed still another enemy, viz. a night-prowling owl of sharp beaks, named Chandraka, sitting on a branch of the banyan tree.

5.4 गतस्य विषयं तत्र नकुलोलूकयोस्तथा ।
अथास्यासीदियं चिन्ता तत्प्रात्य सुमहद्भयम् ॥ 12.138.33
gatasya visayam tatra nakulolukayostatha
athasyasidiyam cinta tatprapya sumahadbhayam
—12.138.33

Simple meaning—Having become an object of prey by two more enemies (the mongoose and the owl), that is, three enemies including the cat, the mouse, in great alarm, began to ponder over his plight.

आपद्यस्यां सुकष्टायां मरणे प्रत्युपस्थिते ।
समन्ताद् भय उत्पन्ने कथं कार्यं हितैषिणा ॥ 12.138.34
apadyasyam sukastayam marane pratyupasthite
samantad bhaya utpanne katham karyam hitaisina
—12.138.34

Simple meaning—The mouse mused but did not panic, "A great calamity has suddenly befallen me. How should I protect myself?"

गतं मां सहसा भूमिं नकुलो भक्षयिष्यति ।
उलूकश्चेह तिष्ठन्तं मार्जारः पाशसंक्षयात् ॥ 12.138.37
gatam mam sahasa bhumim nakulo bhaksayisyati
ulukasceha tisthantam marjarah pasasanksayat
—12.138.37

Simple meaning—"If I try to run, the mongoose will eat me up. If I stay on the net, the owl will kill me by his sharp beaks. If I go inside the net, the cat will devour me".

मूषिकः सर्वतो रुद्धः सर्वत्र भयदर्शनः । 12.138.35
न धर्मकुशलः प्राज्ञः सम्मोहं गन्तुमर्हति ॥
करिष्ये जीवितं यत्नं यावद् युक्त्या प्रतिग्रहाद् ॥ 12.138.38

musikah sarvato ruddhah sarvatra bhayadarsanah
—12.138.35
na dharmakusalah prajnah sammoham gantumarhati
karisye jivitam yatnam yavad yuktya pratigrahad
—12.138.38

Simple meaning—"Howsoever serious the situation might be, and inspite of being surrounded by three enemies, an intelligent being like me should not become dumb-founded. And the only way I can possibly save myself is to seek the cooperation of one of the three enemies".

न त्वन्यामिह मार्जाराद् गतिं पश्यामि साम्प्रतम् ।
विषमस्थो ह्ययं शत्रुः कृत्यं चास्य महन्मया ॥ 12.138.41

na tvanyamiha marjarad gatim pasyami sampratam
visamastho hyayam satruh krityam casya mahanmaya
—12.138.41

Simple meaning—"After analysing all the options, I think my best bet is to make peace with the cat. Although he is my perpetual enemy, yet at this point of time, he himself is trapped into the hunter's net and I have the capability to release him from that trap".

कदाचिद् व्यसनं प्राप्य संधि कुर्यान्मया सह ।
ज्ञानिना सन्निकृष्टस्य शत्रोरपि परिग्रहः ।
कार्य इत्याहुराचार्या विषमे जीवितार्थिना ॥ 12.138.45

kadacid vyasanam prapya sandhi kuryanmaya saha
jnanina sannikristasya satrorapi parigrahah
karya ityahuracarya visame jivitarthina
—12.138.45

Simple meaning—"May be, if I offer to get him out of the trap, the cat might make peace with me. The most famous scholars have advised that, even those who are enemies in normal times, should join hands in times of crisis. At the moment, I as well as the cat, facing death separately, can hope to stay alive by joining hands".

5.5 ततोऽर्थगतितत्त्वज्ञः संधिविग्रहकालवित् ।
सान्त्वपूर्वमिदं वाक्यं मार्जारं मूषिकोऽब्रवीत् ॥ 12.138. 49

tatorthagatitattvajnah sandhivigrahakalavit
santvapurvamidam vakyam marjaram musikobravit
—12.138.49

Simple meaning—The wise mouse, having prepared, in his mind, a rescue plan for himself and the cat, spoke to the cat in a sweet and sympathetic tone.

सौहृदेनाभिभाषे त्वां कच्चिन् मार्जार जीवसि ।
जीवितं हि तवेच्छामि श्रेयः साधारणं हि नौ ॥ 12.138.50

sauhridenabhibhase tvam kaccin marjara jivasi
jivitam hi tavecchami sreyah sadharanam he nau
—12.138.50

Simple meaning—The mouse said, "My dear cat, I speak to you as a friend. I hope you are still alive. I want to make genuine effort so that you remain alive, particularly because you and I have a common escape route from this crisis".

न ते सौम्य भयं कार्यं जीविष्यसि यथासुखम् ।
अहं त्वामुद्धरिष्यामि यदि मां न जिघांससि ॥ 12.138.51

na te saumya bhayam karyam jivisyasi yathasukham
aham tvamuddharisyami yadi mam na jighamsasi
—12.138.51

Simple meaning—"My dear cat, if you give up the desire to eat me up, I will cut open the hunter's net and enable you to escape. Then you will live happily thereafter. So you need not be afraid that the hunter will kill you".

इदं हि नकुलोलूकं पापबुद्ध्याभिसंस्थितम् ।
न धर्षयति मार्जार तेन मे स्वस्ति साम्प्रतम् ॥ 12.138.54

idam hi nakulolukam papabuddhyabhisamsthitam
na dharsayati marjara tena me svasti sampratam
—12.138.54

Simple meaning—"My dear cat, you might be wondering why I am thinking of this plan to obtain your release from the net. The reason is that I need your help to protect me from the owl and the mongoose".

सतां साप्तपदं मैत्रं स सखा मेऽसि पंडितः ।
सांवास्यकं करिष्यामि नास्ति ते भयमद्य वै ॥ 12.138.56

satam saptapadam maitram sa sakha mesi panditah
samvasyakam karisyami nasti te bhayamadya vai
—12.138.56

Simple meaning—"My dear cat, noble beings become friends if they walk seven steps together. You and I have lived here for a long time, therefore I consider you as my noble friend. My plan to obtain your release from the net, is a part of my duty towards you as a friend. Therefore, you should drive away all fear from your heart".

यस्मिन्नाश्वासते कश्चिद् यश्च नाश्वसिति क्वचित् ।
न तौ धीराः प्रशंसन्ति नित्यमुद्विग्नमानसौ ॥ 12.138.59

yasminnasvasate kascid yasca nasvasiti kvacit
na tau dhirah prasamsanti nityamudvignamanasau
—12.138.59

Simple meaning—"My dear cat, to trust each other is an essential part of friendship. If two beings do not trust each other, then they are considered ignoble by wise people. You and I are noble friends because we trust each other".

ईदृशो नौ समायोगो भविष्यति सुविस्तरः ।
अहं त्वां तारयिष्यामि मां च त्वं तारयिष्यसि ॥ 12.138.63

idriso nau samayogo bhavisyati suvistarah
aham tvam tarayisyami mam ca tvam tarayisyasi
—12.138.63

Simple meaning—"My dear cat, our mutual trust and cooperation will be long-lasting. Because of this, I will obtain your release from the hunter's net, and you will protect me from the owl and the mongoose".

5.6 एवमुक्त्वा तु पलितस्तमर्थमुभयोर्हितम् ।
हेतुमद् ग्रहणीयं च कालापेक्षी न्यवेक्ष्य च ॥ 12.138.64
evamuktva tu palitastamarthamubhayorhitam
hetumad grahaniyam ca kalapeksi nyaveksya ca
—12.138.64

Simple meaning—The most appealing aspect of the argument put forth by the mouse was that it showed the way how mutual help could lead to the rescue of both of them, from the crisis situation. Having clearly laid out the plan, the mouse waited for the cat's response.

बुद्धिमान् वाक्यसम्पन्नस्तद्वाक्यमनुवर्णयन् ।
स्वामवस्थां समीक्ष्याथ साम्नैव प्रत्यपूजयत् ॥ 12.138.66
मूषिकं मन्दमुद्वीक्ष्य मार्जारो लोमशोऽब्रवीत् ॥ 12.138.67
buddhiman vakyasampannastadvakyamanuvarnayan
svamavastham samiksyatha samnaiva pratyapujayat
—12.138.66
musikam mandamudviksya marjaro lomasobravit
—12.138.67

Simple meaning—The cat was as intelligent as the mouse. He considered every aspect of the plan and felt happy that the peace treaty between the two of them was aimed at doing good to both of them. He developed a worshipful attitude towards the mouse, and then started expressing his concurrence with the plan put forward by the mouse.

5.7 नन्दामि सौम्य भद्रं ते यो मां जीवितुमिच्छसि ॥ 12.138.68
अहं हि भृशमापन्नस्त्वमापन्नतरो मम।
द्वयोरापन्नयोः सन्धिः क्रियतां मा चिराय च ॥ 12.138.69
nandami saumya bhadram te yo mam jivitumicchasi
—12.138.68

aham hi bhrisamapannastvamapannataro mama
dvayorapannayoh sandhih kriyatam ma ciraya ca
—12.138.69

Simple meaning—The cat said, "My dear mouse, I bow to you, and am grateful that you want to keep me alive. As things stand, I am entangled in a crisis and you too are similarly entangled. It is obvious, therefore, that we two should immediately enter into a peace treaty, to implement the rescue plan that you have proposed, for the benefit of both of us".

न्यस्तमानोऽस्मि भक्तोऽस्मि शिष्यस्त्वद्धितकृत् तथा ।
निदेशवशवर्ती च भवन्तं शरणं गतः ॥ 12.138.71
nyastamanosmi bhaktosmi sisyastvaddhitakrit tatha
nidesavasavarti ca bhavantam saranam gatah
—12.138.71

Simple meaning—"My dear mouse, I feel crest-fallen now, but you will lift me up. Therefore, as a devotee and a disciple, I will whole-heartedly do good to you. Whatever advice you give me, I will act accordingly".

5.8 इत्येवमुक्तः पलितो मार्जारं वशमागतम् ।
वाक्यं हितमुवाचेदमभिनीतार्थमर्थवित् ॥ 12.138.72
ityevamuktah palito marjaram vasamagatam
vakyam hitamuvacedamabhinitarthamarthavit
—12.138.72

Simple meaning—After getting such a worshipful response from the cat, the wise mouse explained what precisely he wanted the cat to do, as a part of the plan.

अहं त्वानुप्रवेक्ष्यामि नकुलान्मे महद् भयम् ।
त्रायस्व भो मा वधीस्त्वं शक्तोऽस्मि तव रक्षणे ॥ 12.138.74
aham tvanupraveksyami nakulanme mahad bhayam
trayasva bho ma vadhistvam saktosmi tava raksane
—12.138.74

Simple meaning—The mouse said to the cat, "My dear friend, this is what we need to do immediately. To save myself from the mongoose, I will enter the net. But, my dear friend, don't eat me up. Protect me and keep me alive, because only then I can cut the strings of the net and pave the way for your release".

उलूकाच्चैव मां रक्ष क्षुद्रः प्रार्थयते हि माम् ।
अहं छेस्यामि ते पाशान् सखे सत्येन ते शपे ॥ 12.138.75

ulukaccaiva mam raksa ksudrah prarthayate hi mam
aham chesyami te pasan sakhe satyena te sape
—12.138.75

Simple meaning—"Furthermore, my dear friend, you will protect me from the owl too. Once I find myself secure, I will cut the strings of the net in which you are entrapped. I swear by Truth, my dear friend".

5.9 तद्वचः संगतं श्रुत्वा लोमशो युक्तमर्थवत् ।
हर्षादुद्वीक्ष्य पलितं स्वागतेनाभ्यपूजयत् ॥ 12.138.76
तं सम्पूज्याथ पलितं मार्जारः सौहृदे स्थितः ।
स विचिन्त्याब्रवीद् धीरः प्रीतस्त्वरित एव च ॥ 12.138.77

tadvacah sangatam srutva lomaso yuktamarthavat
harsaduduviksya palitam svagatenabhyapujayat
—12.138.76

tam sampujyatha palitam marjarah sauhride sthitah
sa vicintyabravid dhirah pritastvarita eva ca
—12.138.77

Simple meaning—The cat was convinced that the plan put forward by the mouse was perfect. He saw in it a ray of hope for his own release and the only obligation on his part was to protect the mouse. He felt happy that a venerable being like the mouse is his friend, at such a critical moment in his life. Filled with such firm conviction about the usefulness of the peace treaty, the cat prepared himself mentally, to make a long statement, admiring the mouse for the initiative that he had taken.

5.10 शीघ्रमागच्छ भद्रं ते त्वं मे प्राणसमः सखा ।
तव प्राज्ञ प्रसादाद्धि प्रायः प्राप्स्यामि जीवितम् ॥ 12.138.78

sighramagaccha bhadram te tvam me pranasamah sakha
tava prajna prasadaddhi prayah prapsyami jivitam
—12.138.78

Simple meaning—The cat said to the mouse, "My dearest friend, come into the net quickly. I will welcome you and protect you from the owl and the mongoose. In fact, you are as dear to me as my own life. It is because of your wisdom and grace that I can hope to stay alive".

यद् यदेवंगतेनाद्य शक्यं कर्तुं मया तव ।
यदाज्ञापय कर्तास्मि संधिरेवास्तु नौ सखे ॥ 12.138.79
yad yadevangatenadya sakyam kartum maya tava
yadajnapaya kartasmi sandhirevastu nau sakhe
—12.138.79

Simple meaning—"I want that the peace treaty between us should stay firm. I had lost hope of remaining alive and so I honour you for extending a helping hand to me at such a critical juncture. I too, on my part, want to reciprocate. So please tell me what I can do to help you, not only now, but in future too".

अस्मात् तु संकटान्मुक्त: समित्रगणबान्धव: ।
सर्वकार्याणि कर्ताहं प्रियाणि च हितानि च ॥ 12.138.80
asmat tu sankatanmuktah samitraganabandhavah
sarvakaryani kartaham priyani ca hitani ca
—12.138.80

Simple meaning—"Once I get my release from this crisis, I, along with my friends and relations, will keep on doing those things which are beneficial to you and which add to your happiness".

मुक्तश्च व्यसनादस्मात् सौम्याहमपि नाम ते ।
प्रीतिमुत्पादयेयं च प्रीतिकर्तुश्च सत्क्रियाम् ॥ 12.138.81
muktasca vyasanadasmat saumyahamapi nama te
pritimutpadayeyam ca pritikartusa satkriyam
—12.138.81

Simple meaning—"I will always remember that it was you who came to my help when I needed it most, and I am sure my gratefulness and desire to reciprocate, will gladden your heart".

प्रत्युपकुर्वन् बह्वपि न भाति
पूर्वोपकारिणा तुल्यः ।
एकः करोति हि कृते
निष्कारणमेव कुरुतेऽन्यः ॥ 12.138.82

pratyapakurvan bahvapi na bhati
purvopakarina tulyah
ekah karoti hi krite
niskaranameva kurutenyah

—12.138.82

Simple meaning—The cat concluded by admiring helpers who take the initiative, "I firmly believe that, when two friends help each other, the one who took the initiative is more honourable. The one who reciprocates has a lower place, irrespective of what he or she might do. The spontaneity of the one who took the initiative, uplifts the quality of that contribution, in comparison to the honour received by the one who reciprocates". [1]

5.11 ग्राहयित्वा तु तं स्वार्थं मार्जारं मूषिकस्तथा ।
प्रविवेश तु विश्रभ्य क्रोडमस्य कृतागसः ॥ 12.138.83

grahayitva tu tam svartham marjaram musikastatha
pravivesa tu visrabhya krodamasya kritagasah

—12.138.83

Simple meaning—The mouse, having received firm assurances, entered the net and trustfully crouched beneath the cat's body.

एवमाश्वासितो विद्वान् मार्जारेण स मूषिकः।
मार्जारोरसि विस्त्रब्धः सुष्वाप पितृमातृवत् ॥ 12.138.84

evamasvasito vidvan marjarena sa musikah
marjarorasi visrabdhah susvapa pitrimatrivat

—12.138.84

Simple meaning—The wise mouse demonstrated his complete trust in what the cat had said, and happily laid himself under the breast of the cat as if is were the lap of his mother or father.

5.12 लीनं तु तस्य गात्रेषु मार्जारस्य च मूषिकम् ।
दृष्ट्वा तौ नकुलोलूकौ निराशौ प्रत्यपद्यताम् ॥ 12.138.85
linam tu tasya gatresu marjarasya ca musikam
dristva tau nakulolukau nirasau pratyapadyatam
—12.138.85

Simple meaning—When the owl as well as the mongoose saw that the mouse, being under the breast of the cat, was unassailable, then both of them were deeply disappointed.

दृष्ट्वा तयोः परां प्रीतिं विस्मयं परमं गतौ ॥ 12.138.86
उलूकनकुलौ तूर्णं जग्मतुस्तौ स्वमालयम् ॥ 12.138.88
dristva tayoh param pritim vismayam paramam gatau
—12.138.86
ulukanakulau turnam jagmatustau svamalayam
—12.138.88

Simple meaning—The fact that the cat and the mouse are now close friends, caused surprise and bewilderment, to the owl as well as to the mongoose. Both of them then thought it would be better for them to go elsewhere in search of food. (From the viewpoint of the mouse, this meant protection from two enemies).

5.13 लीनः स तस्य गात्रेषु पलितो देशकालवित् ।
चिच्छेद पाशान् नृपते कालापेक्षी शनैः शनैः ॥ 12.138.89
linah sa tasya gatresu palito desakalavit
ciccheda pasan nripate kalapekshi sanaih sanaih
—12.138.89

Simple meaning—Having saved himself from the owl and the mongoose, the wise mouse got busy in working out the right strategy in regard to the time he should take for cutting the strings of the net in which the cat was trapped. He decided that he should do this rather slowly.

5.14 अथ बंधपरिक्लिष्टो मार्जारो वीक्ष्य मूषिकम् ।
छिन्दन्तं वै तदा पाशानत्वरन्तं त्वरान्वितः ॥ 12.138.90
तमत्वरन्तं पलितं पाशानां छेदने तथा ।
संचोदयितुमारेभे मार्जारो मूषिकं तदा ॥ 12.138.91

atha bandhapariklisto marjaro viksya musikam
chindantam vai tada pasanatvarantam tvaranvitah
—12.138.90

tamatvarantam palitam pasanam chedane tatha
sancodayitumarebhe marjaro musikam tada
—12.138.91

Simple meaning—On the other hand, the cat wanted the mouse to cut the strings quickly because he felt uneasy inside the net. He got impatient at the slow speed of the mouse, and, hoping to get the work expedited, he (*i.e.* the cat) spoke.

किं सौम्य नातित्वरसे किं कृतार्थोऽवमन्यसे ।
छिन्धि पाशानमित्रघ्न पुरा श्वपच एति च ॥ 12.138.92

kim saumya natitvarase kim kritarthovamanyase
chindhi pasanamitraghna pura svapaca eti ca
—12.138.92

Simple meaning—The cat said to the mouse, "My dear friend, I wonder why you are not cutting the strings quickly. Is it that, after getting your own work done, you are paying inadequate attention to my work? Keep in mind, my dear, the need for urgency, because the hunter will be here soon".

5.15 इत्युक्तस्त्वरता तेन मतिमान् पलितोऽब्रवीत् ।
मार्जारमकृतप्रज्ञं पथ्यमात्महितं वचः ॥ 12.138.93

ityuktastvarata tena matiman palitobravit
marjaramakritaprajnam pathyamatmahitam vacah
—12.138.93

Simple meaning—It was clear that the cat was getting impatient. Furthermore, the intelligent mouse also felt that the cat did not fully grasp the intricate nature of the relationship between the two of them. He therefore decided to explain in detail why his speed of work at that time was rather slow, but still appropriate.

तूष्णीं भव न ते सौम्य त्वरा कार्या न सम्भ्रमः ।
वयमेवात्र कालज्ञा न कालः परिहास्यते ॥ 12.138.94

tusnim bhava na te saumya tvara karya na sambhramah
vayamevatra kalajna na kalah parihasyate

—12.138.94

Simple meaning—The mouse said to the cat, "My dearest friend, please do not get impatient. I fully understand the need for urgency, but, within the time limit linked with the hunter's arrival, there is another consideration which I want you to understand. After you grasp that viewpoint, you will not criticize me for my slow speed of work".

अकाले कृत्यमारब्धं कर्तुर्नार्थाय कल्पते।
तदेव काल आरब्धं महतेऽर्थाय कल्पते ॥ 12.138.95

akale krityamarabdham karturnarthaya kalpate
tadeva kala arabdham mahaterthaya kalpate

—12.138.95

Simple meaning—"My dearest friend, I guarantee that I will cut the chains of the net before the arrival of the hunter, but within this time limit, I know which particular speed is the most appropriate. Sages have declared that, if an act is begun at the wrong time, it never serves the purpose because it is completed at the wrong time too. The same act, if begun at the right time, proves to be great because it is completed at the right time too".

अकाले विप्रमुक्तान्मे त्वत्त एव भयं भवेत् ।
तस्मात् कालं प्रतीक्षस्व किमिति त्वरसे सखे ॥ 12.138.96

akale vipramuktanme tvatta eva bhayam bhavet
tasmat kalam pratiksasva kimiti tvarase sakhe

—12.138.96

Simple meaning—"My dearest friend, please excuse me if I point out the problem which could arise if I work at a faster speed. If I complete my work before I can see the hunter walking towards us, from a little distance, then you may not be so keen to run away from this place and I may feel unsafe in your presence. Therefore, my dearest friend, have patience and wait for the right moment".

यदा पश्यामि चाण्डालमायान्तं शस्त्रपाणिनम्।
ततश्छेत्स्यामि ते पाशान् प्राप्ते साधारणे भये ॥ 12.138.97
तस्मिन् काले प्रमुक्तस्त्वं तरुमेवाधिरोक्ष्यसे ।
न हि ते जीवितादन्यात् किंचित् कृत्यं भविष्यति ॥ 12.138.98
ततो भवत्यपक्रान्ते त्रस्ते भीते च लोमश ।
अहं बिलं प्रेवक्ष्यामि भवान् शाखां भजिष्यति ॥ 12.138.99

yada pasyami candalamayantam sastrapaninam
tataschetsyami te pasan prapte sadharane bhaye
—12.138.97

tasmin kale pramuktastvam tarumevadhiroksyase
na hi te jivitadanyat kincit krityam bhavisyati
—12.138.98

tato bhavatyapakrante traste bhite ca lomasa
aham bilam praveksyami bhavan sakham bhajisyati
—12.138.99

Simple meaning—"My dearest friend, I will plan the speed of my work in such a way that the final string of the net will be cut when I see the hunter walking towards us, from a little distance. At that moment, both you and I will be in a hurry to get away from this place. At the sight of the hunter, the only thing that you will think of, will be to save your life by climbing up the tree. And I too, feeling safe in that situation, will enter my hole. Therefore, my dearest friend, allow me to follow this plan, which is in the best interests, of you as well as me".

5.16 एवमुक्तस्तु मार्जारो मूषिकेणात्मनो हितम् ।
वचनं वाक्यतत्त्वज्ञो जीवितार्थी महामतिः ॥ 12.138.100
अथात्मकृत्ये त्वरितः सम्यक् प्रश्रितमाचरन् ।
उवाच लोमशो वाक्यं मूषिकं चिरकारिणम् ॥ 12.138.101

evamuktastu marjaro musikenatmano hitam
vacanam vakyatattvajno jivitarthi mahamatih
—12.138.100
athatmakritye tvaritah samyak prasritamacaran
uvaca lomaso vakyam musikam cirakarinam
—12.138.101

Simple meaning—After hearing all this, the cat was convinced that he will be saved by the mouse, but only at the last moment, that is, when the hunter is about to come. His request for expediting the cutting of the strings, was not accepted by the mouse. His (*i.e.* the cat's) mood, at that time, was a mixture of unease and reconciliation, and he prepared himself mentally, to expain this to the mouse.

न ह्येवं मित्रकार्याणि प्रीत्या कुर्वन्ति साधवः ।
यथा त्वं मोक्षितः कृच्छ्रात् त्वरमाणेन वै मया ॥ 12.138.102
तथा हि त्वरमाणेन त्वया कार्यं हितं मम ।
यत्नं कुरु महाप्रज्ञ यथा रक्षाऽवयोर्भवेत् ॥ 12.138.103

na hyevam mitrakaryani pritya kurvanti sadhavah
yatha tvam moksitah kricchrat tvaramanena vai maya
—12.138.102
tatha hi tvaramanena tvaya karyam hitam mama
yatnam kuru mahaprajna yatha raksavayorbhavet
—12.138.103

Simple meaning—The cat said to the mouse, "My dear friend, you and I became friends after promising to help each other. A good friend takes pleasure in doing quickly, what the other friend wants. Remember that I protected you immediately from the owl and the mongoose. I expect the same from you too. Of course, I understand that you have to safeguard your interests too, while helping me".

अथवा पूर्ववैरं त्वं स्मरन् कालं जिहीर्षसि ।
पश्य दुष्कृतकर्मंस्तवं व्यक्तमायुःक्षयं तव ॥ 12.138.104
यदि किंचिन्मयाज्ञानात् पुरस्ताद् दुष्कृतं कृतम् ।
न तन्मनसि कर्तव्यं क्षामये त्वां प्रसीद मे ॥ 12.138.105

athava purvavairam tvam smaran kalam jihirsasi
pasya duskritakarmamstvam vyaktamayuhksayam tava
—12.138.104

yadi kincinmayajnanat purastad duskritam kritam
na tanmanasi kartavyam ksamaye tvam prasida me
—12.138.105

Simple meaning—"It seems to me that, even after we became friends, you sometimes think of the earlier time when we were enemies. It is in your interest, not to do so. But I leave it to you to take the final decision about your plan of action. Furthermore, please excuse me if I said or did anything wrong, because of my limited understanding of the complicated relationship between you and me".

5.17 तमेवंवादिनं प्राज्ञः शास्त्रबुद्धिसमन्वितः ।
उवाचेदं वचः श्रेष्ठं मार्जारं मूषिकस्तदा ॥ 12.138.106

tamevamvadinam prajnah sastrabuddhisamanvitah
uvacedam vacah srestham marjaram musikastada
—12.138.106

Simple meaning—Intellectually, the mouse was superior to the cat. He therefore explained once more why his (*i.e.* the mouse's) plan was in the best interests of both of them.

श्रुतं मे तव मार्जार स्वमर्थं परिगृह्णतः ।
ममापि त्वं विजानासि स्वमर्थं परिगृह्णतः ॥ 12.138.107

srutam me tava marjara svamartham parigrihnatah
mamapi tvam vijanasi svamartham parigrihnatah
—12.138.107

Simple meaning—The mouse said to the cat, "My dearest friend, although we promised to help each other, yet it is obvious that your first priority is to safeguard your own interest, and similarly, my first priority is to safeguard my own interest".

यन्मित्रं भीतवत्साध्यं यन्मित्रं भयसंहितम् ।
सुरक्षितव्यं तत् कार्यं पाणिः सर्पमुखादिव ॥ 12.138.108

yanmitram bhitavatsadhyam yanmitram bhayasamhitam
suraksitavyam tat karyam panih sarpamukhadiva
—12.138.108

Simple meaning—"My dearest friend, you should recognize that, friendship started in times of crisis, is inherently different from friendship started in normal times. When I made the offer of friendship to you, I was face-to-face with a crisis, and you too accepted my offer because you yourself were entangled in a crisis. Under such special circumstances, each of us has to safeguard one's own interest, while fulfilling the obligations that arise from friendship. A parallel situation occurs when a snake-charmer takes care of a snake, and at the same time, protects himself from snake-bite".

कृत्वा बलवता संधिमात्मानं यो न रक्षति ।
अपथ्यमिव तद् भुक्तं तस्य नार्थाय कल्पते ॥ 12.138.109

kritva balavata sandhimatmanam yo na raksati
apathyamiva tad bhuktam tasya narthaya kalpate
—12.138.109

Simple meaning—"My dearest friend, one more point about our friendship, although obvious, needs to be pointed out to you, viz. that I am weaker than you. The practical implication of this is that, special steps to safeguard one's interests, are needed to be taken by me (but not by you)".

छिन्नं तु तन्तुबाहुल्यं तन्तुरेकोऽवशेषितः ।
छेत्स्याम्यहं तमप्याशु निवृतो भव लोमश ॥ 12.138.113
तस्मिन्कालेऽपि च भवान् दिवाकीर्तिर्भयार्दितः ।
मम न ग्रहणे शक्तः पलायनपरायणः ॥ 12.138.112

chinnam tu tantubahulyam tanturekovasesitah
chetsyamyaham tamapyasu nivrito bhava lomasa
—12.138.113

tasminkalepi ca bhavan divakirtirbhayarditah
mama na grahane saktah palayanaparayanah
—12.138.112

Simple meaning—"My dearest friend, I have already cut down most of the strings of the net, and I want to reassure you that I will definitely cut down the few strings that remain, before the arrival of the hunter. So please drive away all fear from your mind, and let no trace of it remain to bother you. Finally, please recall what I told you about the best speed of my work - I will complete my work only when I see the hunter from a little distance, because at that time, as soon as you are free, you will be anxious to protect yourself from the hunter and will climb the tree, devoting no attention at all to grabbing me".

5.18 तयो: संवदतोरेवं तथैवापन्नयोर्द्वयो: ।
क्षयं जगाम सा रात्रिर्लोमशं त्वाविशद् भयम् ॥ 12.138.114

tayoh samvadatorevam tathaivapannayordvayoh
ksayam jagama sa ratrirlomasam tvavisad bhayam
—12.138.114

Simple meaning—In this way, while the cat and the mouse talked to each other, about the various questions related to their crisis, the long hours of the night passed off. Inspite of the assurance given by the mouse, the cat was unable to drive away the fear from his mind.

5.19 तत: प्रभातसमये मलिनो घोरदर्शन: ।
परिघो नाम चाण्डाल: शस्त्रपाणिरदृश्यत ॥ 12.138.116

tatah prabhatasamaye malino ghoradarsanah
parigho nama candalah sastrapaniradrisyata
—12.138.116

Simple meaning—Finally, the dark hours of the night gave way to morning, and the cat as well as the mouse, saw at a little distance, the hunter, with arms in hand, walking towards the net, with a view to taking control of the animals that were expected to be entrapped in it during the night.

तं दृष्ट्वा यमदूताभं मार्जारस्त्रस्तचेतन: ।
उवाच वचनं भीत: किमिदानीं करिष्यसि ॥ 12.138.117
ततश्चिच्छेद तं पाशं मार्जारस्य च मूषिक: ॥ 12.138.121

tam dristva yamadutabham marjarastrastacetanah
uvaca vacanam bhitah kimidanim karisyasi
—12.138.117

tatasciccheda tam pasam marjarasya ca musikah
—12.138.121

Simple meaning—To the cat, the hunter was the messenger of Death. With heightened fear, the cat said to the mouse, "The moment of action has arrived". And the mouse replied, "No delay on my part - it is done".

5.20 विप्रमुक्तोऽथ मार्जारस्तमेवाभ्यपतद् द्रुमम् ।
बिलं विवेश पलितः शाखां लेभे स लोमशः ॥ 12.138.122
स तस्मात् सम्भ्रमावर्तान्मुक्तो घोरेण शत्रुणा ॥ 12.138.123
vipramuktotha marjarastamevabhyapatad drumam
bilam vivesa palitah sakham lebhe sa lomasah
—12.138.122
sa tasmat sambhramavartanmukto ghorena satruna
—12.138.123

Simple meaning—As soon as the cat heard the word "Done", he freed himself from the net and climbed up the tree. The mouse then heaved a sigh of relief, because he had managed to protect himself from the third enemy too. In a happy mood, he entered into his hole.

5.21 उन्माथमप्यथादाय चाण्डालो वीक्ष्य सर्वशः।
विहताशः क्षणेनास्ते तस्माद् देशादपाक्रमत् ।
जगाम स स्वभवनं चाण्डालो भरतर्षभ ॥ 12.138.124
unmathamapyathadaya candalo viksya sarvasah
vihatasah ksanenaste tasmad desadapakramat
jagama sa svabhavanam candalo bharatarsabha
—12.138.124

Simple meaning—The cat's release from the net, with the help of the mouse, was sad news for the hunter. He was disappointed to see that the net was empty. He was unaware of the high drama that was enacted, in his net, by the cat and the mouse, during the night. At this point of time in the morning, the hunter had no other option, except going home, empty-handed.

Chapter 6

The Crucial Role of Internal Disunity in State Level Calamity

6.1 There are two chapters in Raja-dharma section of Shanti Parva which discuss calamities at the state level, and point out that these calamities occur more often due to internal problems, rather than due to external causes. In one of these two chapters, Yudhisthira asks a question and Bhisma replies thereto (without telling a story). In the other chapter, while replying to Yudhisthira, Bhisma says, "This problem was discussed between Lord Krishna and Rishi Narada with reference to the internal problems of the Yadavas". In fact, a warning is given in this chapter that, unless the Yadavas settle their internal problems, they will destroy themselves. And this is what actually happened thirty six years later, as narrated in Mausala Parva (*i.e.* Parva No. 16).

6.2 Dialogue between Bhisma and Yudhisthira regarding internal problems of states

युधिष्ठिर उवाच

यथा गणाः प्रवर्धन्ते न भिद्यन्ते च भारत ।

अरींश्च कुर्वन्ति दूरं सुहृदः प्राप्नुवन्ति च ॥ 12.107.7

एतदिच्छाम्यहं श्रोतुं निखिलेन परन्तप ॥ 12.107.9

yudhisthira uvaca

yatha ganah pravardhante na bhidyante ca bharata

arinsca kurvanti duram suhridah prapnuvanti ca

12.107.7

etadicchamyaham srotum nikhilena parantapa
—12.107.9

Simple meaning—Yudhisthira said to Bhisma, "Respected grandfather, please tell me how states can flourish. Is it necessary for this purpose that they avoid internal conflicts? If they do so, then they should be able to expand their circle of friends, and their enemies will think twice before bothering them".

6.3 भीष्म उवाच
गणानां च कुलानां च राज्ञां भरतसत्तम ।
वैरसंदीपनावेतौ लोभामर्षो नराधिप ॥ 12.107.10
bhisma uvaca
gananam ca kulanam ca rajnam bharatasattama
vairasandipanavetau lobhamarso naradhipa
—12.107.10

Simple meaning—Bhisma said to Yudhisthira, "Disunity and antagonism are caused by greed and anger. Such problems occur quite frequently, within states, between states, and between extended families too".

लोभमेको हि वृणुते ततोऽमर्षमनन्तरम् ।
तौ क्षयव्ययसंयुक्तावन्योन्यं च विनाशिनौ ॥ 12.107.11
lobhameko hi vrinute tatomarsamanantaram
tau ksayavyayasamyuktavanyonyam ca vinasinau
—12.107.11

Simple meaning—"The trouble starts with greed. If some members of any group become greedy, they try to cheat others, making them angry. Due to mutual antagonism, the two subgroups ultimately destroy each other".

6.4 भेदे गणा विनेशुर्हि भिन्नास्तु सुजयाः परैः ।
तस्मात् संघातयोगेन प्रयतेरन् गणाः सदा ॥ 12.107.14
bhede gana vinesurhi bhinnastu sujayah paraih
tasmat sanghatayogena prayateran ganah sada
—12.107.14

Simple meaning—"The main cause of destruction of a state is disunity among its citizens. Lack of harmonious relationship weakens the state, and that makes it an easy prey for the invaders. Therefore, the secret of success is "unity of purpose agreed to, by all the subgroups of citizens".

6.5 अर्थाश्चैवाधिगम्यन्ते संघातबलपौरुषैः ।
बाह्याश्च मैत्रीं कुर्वन्ति तेषु संघातवृत्तिषु ॥ 12.107.15
arthascaivadhigamyante sanghatabalapaurusaih
bahyasca maitrim kurvanti tesu sanghatavrittisu
—12.107.15

Simple meaning—"The strength of the state lies in unity and joint effort, and that leads to all-round prosperity and progress. Outsiders also want to establish friendly relationship with such a state".

6.6 ज्ञानवृद्धाः प्रशंसन्ति शुश्रूषन्तः परस्परम् ।
विनिवृत्ताभिसंधानाः सुखमेधन्ति सर्वशः ॥ 12.107.16
jnanavriddhah prasamsanti susrusantah parasparam
vinivrittabhisandhanah sukhamedhanti sarvasah
—12.107.16

Simple meaning—"If the philosophy of all the citizens of the state is "to help one another", then the state receives admiration and blessings of wise people. All-round happiness is bound to be the outcome".

प्राज्ञाञ्शूरान् महोत्साहान् कर्मसु स्थिरपौरुषान् ।
मानयन्तः सदा युक्ता विवर्धन्ते गणा नृप ॥ 12.107.20
prajnamsuran mahotsahan karmasu sthirapaurusan
manayantah sada yukta vivardhante gana nripa
—12.107.20

Simple meaning—"Receiving encouragement from community leaders, all the citizens of the state become enthusiastic Karmayogins, thus ensuring all-round advancement of the state".

6.7 आभ्यन्तरं भयं रक्ष्यमसारं बाह्यतो भयम् ।
आभ्यन्तरं भयं राजन् सद्यो मूलानि कृन्तति ॥ 12.107.28

abhyantaram bhayam raksyamasaram bahyato bhayam
abhyantaram bhayam rajan sadyo mulani krintati
—12.107.28

Simple meaning—"The calamity that a state faces, occurs more often due to internal problems, as compared to external causes. In fact, if internal problems are not taken care of, then they cut the roots and make the entire structure shaky, thus creating conditions which can be exploited by external forces".

अकस्मात् क्रोधमोहाभ्यां लोभाद् वापि स्वभावजात् ।
अन्योन्यं नाभिभाषन्ते तत्पराभवलक्षणम् ॥ 12.107.29
akasmat krodhamohabhyam lobhad vapi svabhavajat
anyonyam nabhibhasante tatparabhavalaksanam
—12.107.29

Simple meaning—"In order to face any crisis successfully, the state requires perfect unity among all the citizens. The key to resolve internal conflicts is purposeful dialogue, avoiding anger, obstinacy and greed. Unless all the citizens do this, willingly and gladly, and in a co-ordinated manner, the state will face destruction".

6.8 भेदाच्चैव प्रदानाच्च भिद्यन्ते रिपुभिर्गणाः ।
तस्मात् संघातमेवाहुर्गणानां शरणं महत् ॥ 12.107.31
संघातबलमजेयं प्राप्तव्या तेनापद्मुक्तिः ।
भेदमूलो विनाशो हि भेदमुक्त्या त्वापद्मुक्तिः ॥ 12.107.32
bhedaccaiva pradanacca bhidyante ripubhirganah
tasmat sanghatamevahurgananam saranam mahat
—12.107.31

sanghatabalamajeyam praptavya tenapadmuktih
bhedamulo vinaso hi bhedamuktya tvapadmuktih
—12.107.32

Simple meaning—"The harmonious relationship among all the citizens of the state, has to be unbreakable and unbribable - and that can make the state "unconquerable". That is why, 'bhedamukti' (unbreakable relationship)and 'apadmukti' (calamity - free existence) are practically synonymous expressions".

Dialogue between Lord Krishna and Rishi Narada regarding internal problems of the Yadavas

6.9 युधिष्ठिर उवाच

एवमग्राह्यके तस्मिञ्ज्ञातिसम्बन्धिमण्डले ।
मित्रेष्वमित्रेष्वपि च कथं भावो विभाव्यते ॥ 12.81.1

yudhisthira uvaca
evamagrahyake tasminjnatisambandhimandale
mitresvamitresvapi ca katham bhavo vibhavyate

—12.81.1

Simple meaning—Yudhisthira asked Bhisma, "If kinsmen and relatives become disunited and form two subgroups opposed to each other, then what should be done to bring about unity of purpose in the community as a whole?"

6.10 भीष्म उवाच

अत्राप्युदाहरन्तीममितिहासं पुरातनम् ।
संवादं वासुदेवस्य सुरर्षेर्नारदस्य च ॥ 12.81.2

bhisma uvaca
atrapyudaharantimamitihasam puratanam
samvadam vasudevasya surarsernaradasya ca

—12.81.2

Simple meaning—Bhisma replied to Yudhisthira, "On this topic, I will narrate to you the dialogue that took place between Lord Krishna and Rishi Narada".

6.11 वासुदेव उवाच

नासुहृत् परमं मंत्रं नारदार्हति वेदितुम् ।
अपण्डितो चापि सुहृत् पण्डितो वाप्यनात्मवान् ॥ 12.81.3

vasudeva uvaca
nasuhrit paramam mantram naradarhati veditum
apandito capi suhrit pandito vapyanatmavan

—12.81.3

Simple meaning—Lord Krishna said to Rishi Narada, "Since you have the right qualities-learning and self-discipline-and you are a well-wisher, I want to consult you about the problem created by rival subgroups among the Yadavas".

बलं संकर्षणे नित्यं सौकुमार्यं पुनर्गदे ।
रूपेण मत्तः प्रद्युम्नः सोऽसहायोऽस्मि नारद ॥ 12.81.7
balam sankarsane nityam saukumaryam punargade
rupena mattah pradyumnah sosahayosmi narada
—12.81.7

Simple meaning—"Although I have my elder brother Balarama, younger brother Gada, and my son Pradyumna, yet I have more confidence in you, than in any of them".

स्यातां यस्याहुकाक्रूरौ किं नु दुःखतरं ततः।
यस्य चापि न तौ स्यातां किं नु दुःखतरं ततः ॥ 12.81.10
syatam yasyahukakrurau kim nu duhkhataram tatah
yasya capi na tau syatam kim nu duhkhataram tatah
—12.81.10

Simple meaning—"It is so painful to me (as the well-wisher of the Yadavas) that Ahuka and Akrura, who are so good to others, are antagonistic to each other (they have formed two rival subgroups among the Yadavas)".

ममैवं क्लिश्यमानस्य नारदोभयतः सदा ।
वक्तुमर्हसि यच्छ्रेयो ज्ञातीनामात्मनस्तथा ॥ 12.81.12
mamaivam klisyamanasya naradobhayatah sada
vaktumarhasi yacchreyo jnatinamatmanastatha
—12.81.12

Simple meaning—"Since I want the good of both the subgroups (who are antagonistic to each other), I am caught in the middle. Perhaps you can advise me how I can ensure the good of both the subgroups (*i.e.* the Yadavas as a whole)".

6.12 नारद उवाच

आपदो द्विविधाः कृष्ण स्वकृता यदि वान्यतः । 12.81.13
अक्रूरभोजप्रभवा ह्यापत् कृच्छ्रा स्वकर्मजा ॥ 12.81.14

narada uvaca
apado dvividhah krishna svakrita yadi vanyatah
—12.81.13
akrurabhojaprabhava hyapat kricchra svakarmaja
—12.81.14

Simple meaning—Rishi Narada said to Lord Krishna, "There are two types of calamities, viz. (*a*) created by one self, and (*b*) created by others. In the case of the Yadavas, since Ahuka and Akrura are closely related, the calamity caused by their mutual antagonism, is obviously self - created".

अनायसेन शस्त्रेण मृदुना हृदयच्छिदा ।
जिह्वामुद्धर सर्वेषां परिमृज्यानुमृज्य च ॥ 12.81.19
anayasena sastrena mriduna hridayacchida
jivhamuddhara sarvesam parimrijyanumrijya ca
—12.81.19

Simple meaning—"Since you are caught in the middle, you may consider trying a technique which could possibly bring about a change of heart, on both sides of the conflict (of course, this seems to me too, to be most difficult)".

ज्ञातीनां वक्तुकामानां कटुकानि लघूनि च ।
गिरा त्वं हृदयं वाचं शमयस्व मनांसि च ॥ 12.81.22
jnatinam vaktukamanam katukani laghuni ca
gira tvam hridayam vacam samayasva manamsi ca
—12.81.22

Simple meaning—"When the leaders of opposing subgroups of your community (*i.e.* the Yadavas), both criticize each other and criticize you too, then only sweet words can possibly bring about reconciliation".

6.13 भेदाद् विनाशः संघानां संघमुख्योऽसि केशव ।
यथा त्वां प्राप्य नोत्सीदेदयं संघस्तथा कुरु ॥ 12.81.25
bhedad vinasah sanghanam sanghamukhyosi kesava
yatha tvam prapya notsidedayam sanghastatha kuru
—12.81.25

Simple meaning—"O Krishna, you are the leader of the Yadavas, and you know very well that internal conflicts, if not taken care of, can destroy the whole (Yadava) community. Perhaps you can avert the danger, by using your skill for reconciliation".

> त्वं गुरुः सर्वभूतानां जानीषे त्वं गतागतम् ।
> त्वामासाद्य यदुश्रेष्ठमेधन्ते यादवाः सुखम् ॥ 12.81.30
>
> *tvam guruh sarvabhutanam janise tvam gatagatam*
> *tvamasadya yadusresthamedhante yadavah sukham*
> *—12.81.30*

Simple meaning—"O Krishna, you are the supreme teacher of all human beings, and you know the past, the present, and the future. Under your leadership, the Yadava community has made tremendous progress. I hope and pray that the community will take care of internal conflicts, and not destroy itself".

6.14 Here ends the dialogue between Lord Krishna and Rishi Narada (as reported in Shanti Parva). This dialogue contains a clear warning that, unless the Yadavas put an end to their internal conflicts, they will destroy themselves. And this is what actually happened thirty six years later, as narrated in Mausala Parva (*i.e.* Parva No. 16 of the Mahabharata)[1]

CHAPTER 7

Story of Medhavi's Peace Initiative at the Global Level

7.1 Although Medhavi's story occurs in Moksa-dharma section of Shanti Parva, the fact that he launched a peace initiative to protect the global society from "too much violence", justifies its inclusion in this book on Apad-dharma. The existence of too much violence and selfishness in the global society was considered by Medhavi to be a very serious crisis. He pointed out to his father (who was a traditional teacher) that lack of right education was partly responsible for this. Medhavi's peace initiative, called 'Shanti-yajna' symbolizes a revolutionary approach, and the initial reaction of his father was: 'Is it necessary to depart from the traditional approach?' As soon as his father understood Medhavi's plan of starting a new movement, based on right education, and aimed at bringing about a U-turn in the crisis situation, he (*i.e.* the father) joined that movement. Vyasa, the author of the Mahabharata, considered Medhavi's story as particularly important, so much so that he narrated this story twice, *i.e.* in two different chapters, one at the beginning of Moksa-dharma, and the second one in the middle of Moksa-dharma. We narrate the story in full (giving shloka numbers from both the chapters so as not to overlook either of them).

7.2 Before we start narrating the story, we want to prepare the readers (mentally) for appreciating 'repetitions' in the text. Since Medhavi was keen to make his 'peace initiative' a 'mass movement', he made repetitive pleas from different angles in an attempt to secure the support of different sections of the global society. Underlying all these pleas, there are four main messages which can be given a modernistic expression :

(i) If 'too much violence in the society' is not considered a global calamity by the traditional approach, then there is a serious, anti-social flaw in that approach.

(ii) The younger generation is fully competent to replace the flawed (traditional; anti-social) approach by a new, 'social responsibility' approach which aims at bringing about a U-turn in the global crisis situation, by peaceful methods like right education and inter-faith dialogue.

(iii) An appeal should be made to all the citizens of the world (including those initially opposed to the new approach) to extend their active support to the new, 'social responsibility' approach.

(iv) As soon as the main elements of the new approach start receiving support from social activists, their implementation at the global level should be taken up without any delay.

7.3 युधिष्ठिर उवाच

अतिक्रामति कालेऽस्मिन् सर्वभूतभयावहे ।
किं श्रेय: प्रतिपद्येत तन्मे ब्रूहि पितामहे ॥ 12.277.1

yudhisthira uvaca
atikramati kalesmin sarvabhutabhayavahe
kim sreyah pratipadyeta tanme bruhi pitamahe
—12.277.1

Simple meaning—Yudhisthira asked Bhisma, "Respected grand-father, in a crisis situation when the lives of all the people are threatened, what sort of action can set things right?"

भीष्म उवाच

अत्राप्युदाहरन्तीममितिहासं पुरातनम् ।
पितुः पुत्रेण संवादं तं निबोध युधिष्ठिर ॥ 12.277.2

bhisma uvaca

atrapyudaharantimamitihasam puratanam
pituh putrena samvadam tam nibodha yudhisthira
—12.277.2

Simple meaning—Bhisma replied to Yudhisthira, "I will tell you the story of Medhavi - in ancient times, he discussed with his father, the appropriate plan of action to face a crisis that threatened the entire society".

7.4 द्विजातेः कस्यचित् पार्थ स्वाध्यायनिरतस्य वै ।
बभूव पुत्रो मेधावी मेधावी नाम नामतः ॥ 12.277.3
dvijateh kasyacit partha svadhyayaniratasya vai
babhuva putro medhavi medhavi nama namatah
—12.277.3

Simple meaning—"Medhavi's father was a great scholar and teacher. Medhavi's own intelligence became obvious when he was a young boy. It was a nice coincidence that the name (Medhavi) given to him by his parents was so appropriate (because the word 'Medhavi' means 'intelligent')".

7.5 सोऽब्रवीत् पितरं पुत्रः स्वाध्यायकरणे रतम् ।
मोक्षधर्मार्थकुशलो लोकतत्त्वविचक्षणः ॥ 12.175.4
sobravit pitaram putrah svadhyayakarane ratam
moksadharmarthakusalo lokatattvavicaksanah
—12.175.4

Simple meaning—"Medhavi received excellent, broad-based education, which made him an expert, not only on spiritual ideas, but also on issues related to the social applications of those ideas. After graduation, Medhavi asked his father as to what he should do, to serve the society".

पुत्र उवाच

धीरः किंस्वित् तात कुर्यात् प्रजानन्

क्षिप्रं ह्यायुर्भ्रश्यते मानवानाम् ।
पितस्तदाचक्ष्व यथार्थयोगं
ममानुपूर्व्या येन धर्मं चरेयम् ॥ 12.175.5

putra uvaca
dhirah kimsvit tata kuryat prajanan
ksipram hyayurbhrasyate manavanam
pitastadacaksva yatharthayogam
mamanupurvya yena dharmam careyam

—12.175.5

Simple meaning—Medhavi said to his father, "I notice that people's lives have become so insecure. Now that I have completed my studies, I am keen to do something to set things right. Please advise me what I should do".

7.6 पितोवाच
वेदानधीत्य ब्रह्मचर्येण पुत्र
पुत्रानिच्छेत् पावनार्थं पितृणाम् ।
अग्नीनाधाय विधिवच्चेष्टयज्ञो
वनं प्रविश्याथ मुनिर्बुभूषेत् ॥ 12.175.6

pitovaca
vedanadhitya brahmacaryena putra
putranicchet pavanartham pitrinam
agninadhaya vidhivaccestayajno
vanam pravisyatha munirbubhuset

—12.175.6

Simple meaning—Medhavi's father replied, "My dear son, our family has a long tradition of studying and teaching, and we have been following Varnashrama - dharma, and I advise you to continue the same tradition. Although you already know about the dharmic tradition, still I repeat what it means, viz. Brahmacharya-ashrama (for studies), Grihastha-ashrama (for raising family and for teaching), (Vanaprastha-ashrama) (for semi-retirement), and Samnyasa-ashrama (for complete retirement)".

7.7 पुत्र उवाच

एवमभ्याहते लोके समन्तात् परिवारिते ।
अमोघासु पतन्तीषु किं धीर इव भाषसे ॥ 12.175.7

putra uvaca
evamabhyahate loke samantat parivarite
amoghasu patantisu kim dhira iva bhasase
—12.175.7

Simple meaning—Medhavi said, "Respected father, you advise me to follow the family tradition, as if things are moving on nicely, in the society as a whole. But things are not moving on nicely. It seems to me that the deteriorating social situation has not been taken into account by you, otherwise you would not have advised me to carry on the tradition, as if no new ideas are needed. When people's lives everywhere are endangered by too much violence, how can anyone say "This is not my problem"?"

7.8 पितोवाच

कथमभ्याहतो लोकः केन वा परिवारितः ।
अमोघाः काः पतन्तीह किं नु भीषयसीव माम् ॥ 12.277.8

pitovaca
kathamabhyahato lokah kena va parivaritah
amoghah kah patantiha kim nu bhisayasiva mam
—12.277.8

Simple meaning—Medhavi's father replied, "My dear son, why do you say things that cause fear in my mind? I admit that tradition-following people like me have not taken into account the social situation. So tell me, what sort of problems, in your opinion, the society is facing now, and if you are thinking of departing from tradition, what new things you are planning to do".

7.9 पुत्र उवाच

मृत्युनाभ्याहतो लोको जरया परिवारितः ।
अहोरात्राः पतन्त्येके ननु कस्मान्न बुद्ध्यसे ॥ 12.277.9

putra uvaca
mrityunabhyahato loko jaraya parivaritah
ahoratrah patantyeke nanu kasmanna buddhyase
—12.277.9

Simple meaning—Medhavi said, "Respected father, I am surprised that tradition - bound people like you have paid no attention to the deteriorating social situation. To me, the social crisis is so obvious. People's lives are getting more and more insecure. The condition of old people is becoming particularly difficult. Common people's lives have fallen into a rut and they have nothing to look forward to".

7.10 अमोघा रात्रयश्चापि नित्यमायान्ति यान्ति च ।
यदाहमेतज्जानामि न मृत्युस्तिष्ठतीति ह ।
सोऽहं कथं प्रतीक्षिष्ये जालेनापिहितश्चरन् ॥ 12.175.10

amogha ratrayascapi nityamayanti yanti ca
yadahametajjanami na mritystisthatiti ha
soham katham pratiksisye jalenapihitascaran
—12.175.10

Simple meaning—Medhavi continued, "Respected father, I have ascertained not only the existence of the problem (as stated above), but also that "lack of right education and of right knowledge" is one of the causes of the problem. This means that we are all partly responsible for the social crisis. Equipped with such understanding, how can I not take any remedial action"?

7.11 रात्र्यां रात्र्यां व्यतीतायामायुरल्पतरं यदा ।
गाधोदके मत्स्य इव सुखं विन्देत कस्तदा ॥ 12.175.11

ratryam ratryam vyatitayamayuralpataram yada
gadhodake matsya iva sukham vindeta kastada
—12.175.11

Simple meaning—In this shloka, Medhavi referred to Apad-dharma's story about three fish, out of whom one took advance action (*i.e.* moved to a deeper pond) when the water-level of the pond started going down, the second fish moved out at the last moment, but the third fish took no action at all and was caught. (This story is given in Appendix in this book). Now, the continuation of Medhavi's statement. "Of all the social problems, the one that worries me most is "untimely death of people". Just as the falling water-level of the pond was a cause of worry to the fish who wanted to move to a deeper pond, similarly the decline in people's life-expectation is a cause of worry to me and urges me to take remedial action immediately".

7.12 यस्यां रात्र्यां व्यतीतायां न किंचिच्छुभमाचरेत् ।
तदैव वन्ध्यं दिवसमिति विद्याद् विचक्षणः ।
अनवाप्तेषु कामेषु मृत्युरभ्येति मानवम् ॥ 12.175.12

yasyam ratryam vyatitayam na kincicchubhamacaret
tadaiva vandhyam divasamiti vidyad vicaksanah
anavaptesu kamesu mrityurabhyeti manavam
—12.175.12

Simple meaning—Medhavi continued, "Wise people say that, any day or night, in which no action for the good of the society is done, should be considered as "waste of time". This saying will apply to me also if I delay taking remedial action, because in that case, untimely death of people will remain at too high a level, and I will feel guilty".

7.13 शष्पाणीव विचिन्वन्तमन्यत्रगतमानसम् ।
वृकीवोरणमासाद्य मृत्युरादाय गच्छति ॥ 12.175.13

saspaniva vicinvantamanyatragatamanasam
vrikivoranamasadya mrityuradaya gacchati
—12.175.13

Simple meaning—Medhavi continued, "Wise people have warned and advised us not to be 'anyatragatamanasa', that is, advised us not to lose focus on the main thing that we want to accomplish, because that could result in nonfulfilment of the intended plan". Medhavi supports his argument by saying that "by losing focus on their safety, animals in the forest get killed".

7.14 श्वः कार्यमद्य कुर्वीत पूर्वाह्णे चापराह्णिकम् ।
न हि प्रतीक्षते मृत्युः कृतमस्य न वा कृतम् ॥ 12.277.14
svah karyamadya kurvita purvahne caparahnikam
na hi pratiksate mrityuh kritamasya na va kritam
—12.277.14

Simpe meaning—Medhavi continued, "Wise people have advised that, whatever is kept for being done tomorrow, should be done today, and whatever one thinks of doing in the afternoon, should be done in the forenoon. Following this advice, the remedial action for preventing untimely death of people should be implemented by me immediately".

अद्यैव कुरु यच्छ्रेयो मा त्वां कालोत्यगान्महान् ।
को हि जानाति कस्याद्य मृत्युकालो भविष्यति ॥ 12.277.15
न मृत्युरामन्त्रयते हर्तुकामो जगत्प्रभुः।
अबुद्ध एवाक्रमते मीनान् मीनग्रहो यथा ॥ 12.277.16
adyaiva kuru yacchreyo ma tvam kalotyaganmahan
ko hi janati kasyadya mrityukalo bhavisyati
—12.277.15
na mrityuramantrayate hartukamo jagatprabhuh
abuddha evakramate minan minagraho yatha
—12.277.16

Simple meaning—Medhavi continued, "Wise people have conveyed the divine message, viz. that acts for the good of all should be started today, rather than tomorrow. Therefore, the remedial action for preventing untimely death of people should not be postponed by me. Remember the story of three fish (referred to in shloka 12.175.11 above) - the third fish postponed safety measures and was caught".

7.15 अकृतेष्वेव कार्येषु मृत्युर्वै सम्प्रकर्षति ।
युवैव धर्मशीलः स्यादनित्यं खलु जीवितम् ॥ 12.277.17
akritesveva karyesu mrityurvai samprakarsati
yuvaiva dharmasilah syadanityam khalu jivitam
—12.277.17

Simple meaning—Medhavi continued, "Wise people have advised that acts for the good of all should be accomplished by karmayogins while they are still young. As a young person, I should particularly make sure that the remedial action for preventing untimely death of people is implemented now, rather than later".

7.16 कृते धर्मे भवेत् प्रीतिरपि च सात्त्विकं सुखम् ।
मोहेन हि समाविष्टः पुत्रदारार्थमुद्यतः ॥
कृत्वा कार्यमकार्यं च तुष्टिमेषां प्रयच्छति ॥ 12.277.18
तं पुत्रपशुसम्पन्नं व्यासक्तमनसं नरम् ।
सुप्तं व्याघ्रो मृगमिव मृत्युरादाय गच्छति ॥ 12.277.19

krite dharme bhavet pritirapi ca sattvikam sukham
mohena hi samavistah putradararthamudyatah
kritva karyamakaryam ca tustimesam prayacchati
—12.277.18

tam putrapasusampannam vyasaktamanasam naram
suptam vyaghro mrigamiva mrityuradaya gacchati
—12.277.19

Simple meaning—Medhavi continued, "Bhagvad-Gita has taught us that 'sattvika sukha' (real happiness) can be experienced only by doing acts for the good of all, without attachment.[1] On the other hand, 'rajasi sukha' (worldly people's happiness) that is experienced by helping 'svajanam' (own people), is temporary and unreal because it is accompanied with attachment, and also with selfishness. The plan that I want to follow, viz. implementation of the remedial action for preventing untimely death of people, will pave the way for real happiness, if the work is done without attachment, and also without selfishness".

संचिन्वानकमेवैनं कामानामवितृप्तकम् ।
व्याघ्रः पशुमिवादाय मृत्युरादाय गच्छति ॥ 12.175.20

sancinvanakamevainam kamanamavitriptakam
vyaghrah pasumivadaya mrityuradaya gacchati
—12.175.20

Simple meaning—Medhavi continued, "When I visualize those people who meet untimely death due to too much voilence in the society, I feel immense pain because they are deprived of happiness (that is, of even 'rajasi sukha'). My plan to prevent untimely death of people is a symbol of sympathy and support for those who are thus deprived".

7.17 इदं कृतमिदं कार्यमिदमन्यत् कृताकृतम् ।
एवमीहासमायुक्तं मृत्युरादाय गच्छति ॥ 12.277.21
idam kritamidam karyamidamanyat kritakritam
evamihasamayuktam mrityuradaya gacchati
—12.277.21

Simple meaning—Medhavi continued, "Wise people have advised that statements like 'This part has been done, this part remains to be done, this part is half-done' are a reflection of only half-hearted commitment to one's duty, and should be avoided by karmayogins. I will be guided by such advice when I start implementing the plan to prevent untimely death of people".

7.18 कृतानां फलमप्राप्तं कार्याणां कर्मसंगिनाम् ।
क्षेत्रापणगृहासक्तं मृत्युरादाय गच्छति ॥ 12.277.22
kritanam phalamapraptam karyanam karmasanginam
ksetrapanagrihasaktam mrityuradaya gacchati
—12.277.22

Simple meaning—Medhavi continued, "I feel acute pain to see that people who meet untimely death due to too much violence in the society, suffer on two fronts, viz. *(i)* they suffer due to attachment, and *(ii)* they suffer due to untimely death. Once I succeed in preventing their untimely death, I will advise them to do their work without attachment, as taught by Bhagavad-Gita".

7.19 दुर्बलं बलवन्तं च शूरं भीरुं जडं कविम् ।
अप्राप्तसर्वकामार्थं मृत्युरादाय गच्छति ॥ 12.277.23
durbalam balavantam ca suram bhirum jadam kavim
apraptasarvakamartham mrityuradaya gacchati
-12.277.23

Simple meaning—Medhavi continued, "Out of the large number of people who meet untimely death due to too much violence in the society, some are weak, some are strong, some are dumb, some are intelligent. My plan to prevent untimely death will try to cover all of them, without any type of discrimination".

7.20 मृत्युर्जरा च व्याधिश्च दुःखं चानेककारणम् ।
दृष्ट्वापि पीडितं लोकं किं स्वस्थ इव तिष्टसि ॥ 12.175.24
mrityurjara ca vyadhisca duhkham canekakaranam
dristvapi piditam lokam kim svastha iva tisthasi
—12.175.24

Simple meaning—Medhavi continued, "My respected father, the social crisis is clearly visible in the form of insecurity of life, old people's difficulties, and general problems of ill health and widespread suffering. So far you remained too busy, studying and teaching, so much so that your attention was never drawn to the social problems. Now that you have got a clear picture of the social crisis, together with the causes thereof, kindly change your viewpoint and accept that we are all partly responsible for creating this crisis".

7.21 यो न हिंसति सत्त्वानि मनोवाक्कर्महेतुभिः ।
जीवितार्थापनयनैः प्राणिभिर्न स बद्ध्यते ॥ 12.277.25
yo na himsati sattvani manovakkarmahetubhih
jivitarthapanayanaih pranibhirna sa baddhyate
—12.227.25

Simple meaning—From this shloka onward, Medhavi explained the main points of his plan of action. The first point is "non-violence", about which Medhavi said, "Since insecurity of people's lives is the main symptom of the social crisis, I want to promote the practice of non-violence. I interpret non-violence in the broadest possible sense, viz. not to harm any one, by thought, word, or deed, nor by taking away any one's means of livelihood. Furthermore, the practice of non-violence is usually governed by the law of reciprocity, that is, if you are non-violent to others, then they too are likely to be non-violent to you".

7.22 न मृत्युसेनामायान्तीं जातु कश्चित् प्रबाधते ।
ऋते सत्यमसत् त्याज्यं सत्ये ह्यमृतमाश्रितम् ॥ 12.175.26

na mrityusenamayantim jatu kascit prabadhate
rite satyamasat tyajyam satye hyamritamasritam
—12.175.26

Simple meaning—The second point in Medhavi's plan of action is "truth" as defined in Shanti Parva, for example, in the following shloka -

यद्भूतहितमत्यन्तमेतत् सत्यं मतं मम ॥ 12.329.13

yadbhutahitamatyantametat satyam matam mama
—12.329.13

Simple meaning—Truth represents firm intention to do good to all.

Medhavi had earlier spoken about the importance of doing good to all, in verses 12.175.12 and 12.277.15, but now he highlighted this as the meaning of truth, by saying in verse 12.175.26, "In order to face the army of death (that is, to give the assurance of security to all the people) , truth (*i.e.* firm intention to do good to all)is essential, along with non-violence (as explained in shloka 12.277.25)".

तस्मात् सत्यव्रताचारः सत्ययोगपरायणः ।
सत्यकामः समो दान्तः सत्येनैवान्तकं जयेत् ॥ 12.277.27

tasmat satyavratacarah satyayogaparayanah
satyakamah samo dantah satyenaivantakam jayet
—12.277.27

Simple meaning—This is a continuation of the preceding shloka. Medhavi said, "I will declare my commitment to truth, that is, my firm intention to do good to all". He used the expression 'satya yoga' which can be interpreted as making 'truth' (good of all) an integral part of karma yoga, bhakti yoga and jnana yoga. Furthermore, he used the expression 'satyakama' which can be interpreted as 'desirous of doing good to all'. Similarly, the expression in shloka 12.277.27 "antakam jayet" re-iterates the conviction expressed in the preceding shloka that truth can successfully face the army of death, that is, can give the assurance of security to all the people.

7.23 सोऽहं ह्यहिंस्रः सत्यार्थी कामक्रोधबहिष्कृतः ।
लोकसंहारं संहर्तुं करिष्ये विशिष्टं यज्ञं ॥ 12.175.28

soham hyahimsrah satyarthi kamakrodhabahiskritah
lokasamharam samhartum karisye visistam yajnam
—12.175.28

Simple meaning—Medhavi said, "My movement will be based on truth and non-violence. I will get rid of all my vices like lust, anger, greed and hatred. I want to put an end to violence against mankind, by peaceful means. In short, I want to perform a special type of yajna (to be explained in the next shloka)".

शान्तियज्ञरतो दान्तो ब्रह्मयज्ञे स्थितो सदा ।
वाङ्मनःकर्मयज्ञश्च भविष्यामि सर्वहितः ॥ 12.175.29

santiyajnarato danto brahmayajne sthito sada
vanmanahkarmayajnasca bhavisyami sarvahitah
—12.175.29

Simple meaning—Medhavi continued, "The new yajna will be called 'Shanti - yajna' *i.e.* world peace movement. It can also be called 'brahma yajna' *i.e.* a movement based on oneness of all mankind. Similarly, it can be called 'vanmanahkarmayajna' *i.e.* a movement to help mankind, by thought, word and deed".

नास्ति विद्यासमं चक्षुर्नास्ति सत्यसमं तपः ॥ 12.175.35

nasti vidyasamam caksurnasti satyasamam tapah
—12.175.35

Simple meaning—Medhavi concluded, "The main emphasis of the new movement will be on education - a system of education based on truth *i.e.* which does not teach hatred".

7.24 पुत्रस्यैतद् वचः श्रुत्वा यथाकार्षीत् पिता नृप ॥ 12.175.39

putrasyaitad vacah srutva yathakarsit pita nripa
—12.175.39

Simple meaning—Medhavi's plan was so attractive that his father too agreed to take an active part in it.

7.25 For the 21st century readers, it must be clarified that Shanti - yajna does not mean Havan. It is a multi - dimensional plan of action involving inter-faith dialogue and peace-promoting education.

शान्तिर्धर्मः शान्तिर्वार्ता शान्तिर्विद्या शान्तिः शिक्षा ।
शान्तिर्हि तदा गन्तव्या शान्तिकर्मसमाधिना ॥
santirdharmah santirvarta santirvidya santih siksa
santirhi tada gantavya santikarmasamadhina

Simple meaning—A person can be called a performer of Shanti-yajna, if he or she considers world peace as the goal of dharma, if his or her talks (through inter-faith dialogue as well as other channels) are centered on world peace, if world peace is the aim of his or her education, and if he or she teaches world peace to others too—in short, if all the activities are centered on world peace. As a result of Shanti-yajna of this type, how can world peace remain out of reach?

7.26 Medhavi's story symbolizes what peace-loving citizens of the world could do to promote world peace in the 21st century. But Shanti Parva makes it clear that all the governments also need to adopt appropriate policies.

शान्तिनीतिप्रसाराय वांछितो राजधर्मोऽपि ।
santinitiprasaraya vanchito rajadharmopi

Simple meaning—The citizens' peace initiative (shanti-yajna) needs to be supported by governments too by adopting appropriate policies.

7.27 Raja-dharma section of Shanti Parva has listed twenty five ways in which governments can contribute to the cause of world peace. These are specified in the author's earlier book "World Peace Agenda - Based on Shanti Parva of the Mahabharata." Here it might be enough to draw attention to four basic points.

7.28 The first point is the adoption of a firm anti-war policy.

अयुद्धेनैव विजयं वर्धयेद् वसुधाधिपः ।
जघन्यमाहुर्विजयं युद्धेन च नराधिप ॥ 12.94.1

ayuddhenaiva vijayam vardhayed vasudhadhipah
jaghanyamahurvijayam yuddhena ca naradhipa
—12.94.1

Simple meaning—All the governments should declare that their firm policy is to settle all disputes peacefully, because wars cannot provide a satisfactory solution to any dispute.

7.29 The second point is the adoption of lokasamgraha - policies (lokasamgraha meaning 'good of all').

राज्ञो रहस्यं बोद्धव्यं जयार्थं लोकसंग्रहः ॥ 12.58.19

rajno rahasyam boddhavyam jayartham lokasamgrahah
—12.58.19

Simple meaning—Governments which follow lokasamgraha-policies (lokasamgraha meaning 'good of all') are likely to contribute most to the cause of peace—and this is the most effective link between government policy and world peace.

Shanti Parva has included in 'lokasamgraha', all government programs oriented to *(i)* increase food production, *(ii)* increase employment opportunities in socially useful jobs, *(iii)* improve health services, *(iv)* give assurance of security to all the people by protecting them from the army of death (reference Shloka 12.175.26), *(v)* make special arrangements to satisfy health and psychological needs of old people, *(vi)* raise the status of women in the society, *(vii)* protect the environment, and *(viii)* make revolutionary changes in the education system (more on this in the next para).

7.30 शान्तिसंस्थापनार्थाय वांछिता शिक्षाक्रान्तिर्हि

santisamsthapanarthaya vanchita siksakrantirhi

Simple meaning—Revolutionary changes in the education system are essential for promoting the cause of world peace.

Because of the important role of education, this by itself is listed here as the 'third point'. Strong governmental support should be given to programs which seek to give the right education to all the children (*i.e.* boys as well as girls), and which seek to use education to cultivate right values in the society (including the strengthening of fellow-feeling among the people following different faiths). The governments should officially declare that one of the aims of education will be to prepare the minds of students so that they become fit to be peace-loving citizens of the world. In pursuance of this aim, all the students should be given broad- based education and they should also be taught how to use their knowledge for the benefit of mankind. Such teaching should also emphasize and ensure that no student will use his or her knowledge to destroy world peace. If necessary, the governments may seek technical assistance from UNESCO so that they can plan for all-round educational development (of a revolutionary nature), and also implement such plans as quickly and smoothly as possible. All these ideas are like a lesson drawn from Medhavi's story.

7.31 The fourth point is the adoption of a suitable policy for obtaining the support of religious leaders of all faiths, to the cause of world peace.

शान्तिसंस्थापनार्थाय वांछिता वार्ता धर्माणाम्

santisamsthapanarthaya vanchita varta dharmanam

Simple meaning—Religious leaders of different faiths should use inter-faith dialogue to promote the cause of world peace.

7.32 Although inter-faith dialogues are primarily the responsibility of religious leaders, the governments should act as a catalyst to set in motion such dialogues in an increasing number of places, and also to facilitate the production of a written statement on 'How to establish inter-religious harmony' as one of the outcomes of such dialogues.

Even if some of the religious leaders are initially not enthusiastic about such dialogues, the technique of persuation, following Medhavi's example, should be made use of. The United Nations will be happy to extend their support to such programs.

Part II

Based on Stories from Parvas other than Shanti Parva

CHAPTER 8

How Savitri Brought Her Husband Back to Life

8.1 The crisis that Savitri faced was perhaps the most challenging because she saw the Lord of Death (Yama) taking life out of the body of her husband, Satyavan. At that time, she was alone in the forest. But she did not lose heart. Her inner voice gave her confidence that Yama will reverse his decision and give life back to Satyavan. She therefore kept up her dialogue with Yama, and finally she succeeded. Yama granted her five boons which included (besides Satyavan's life) restoration of eyesight and kingdom to her father-in-law, and happiness to her parents too. Savitri's story is narrated by Rishi Markandeya to Yudhisthira in Vana Parva (*i.e.* when the Pandavas were facing the hardship of forest-life), but it fits neatly into the text of Apad-dharma. In this presentation, we want to include, along with Savitri, her father Ashvapati also (as done by Sri Aurobindo in his famous epic 'Savitri').

8.2 आसीन्मद्रेषु धर्मात्मा राजा परमधार्मिकः ।
ब्रह्मण्यश्च महात्मा च सत्यसंधो जितेन्द्रियः ॥ 3.293.5
यज्वा दानपतिर्दक्षः पौरजानपदप्रियः ।
पार्थिवोऽश्वपतिर्नाम सर्वभूतहिते रतः ॥ 3.293.6
क्षमावाननपत्यश्च सत्यवाग् विजितेन्द्रियः 13.293.7

asinmadresu dharmatma raja paramadharmikah
brahmanyasca mahatma ca satyasandho jitendriyah
—3.293.5

yajva danapatirdaksah paurajanapadapriyah
parthivosvapatirnama sarvabhutahite ratah

—*3.293.6*

ksamavananapatyasca satyavag vijitendriyah

—*3.293.7*

Simple meaning—Once upon a time, long ago, Ashvapati was the king of Madra-desa. His devotion to dharma was perfect. He was a great soul, adhering to truth, and self-disciplined. He honored learned people, shared his wealth with others, and was a strong believer in Karma-yoga. He was always engaged in doing good to all the people, urban as well as rural, and they in turn loved him. Inspite of all the virtues, his happiness was incomplete because he had no children.

8.3 Chandogya Upanisad has admired Ashvapati's administration for providing 'eductation to all'.

न मे स्तेनो जनपदे न कदर्यो न मद्यपः ।
नानाहिताग्निर्नाविद्वान्न स्वैरी स्वैरिणी कुतः ॥ छां.उप. 5.11.5

na me steno janapade na kadaryo na madyapah
nanahitagnirnavidvanna svairi svairini kutah

—*ch. up. 5.11.5*

Simple meaning—This mantra (hymn) describes the happy state of affairs achieved by Ashvapati's administration, the main points being:

(i) there was no thief, no miser, no drunkard
(ii) there was no uneducated
(iii) there was no instance of adulterous affair between men and women

8.4 Although Ashvapati wanted to have a son, Goddess Savitri told him that he will be blessed with a daughter of great effulgence (tejas) who will bring even greater bliss to him than any son could have done. Rishi Markandeya told Yudhisthira why the daughter was given the name 'Savitri':

सावित्र्या प्रीतया दत्ता सावित्र्या हुतया ह्यपि ।
सावित्रीत्येव नामास्याश्चक्रुर्विप्रास्तथा पिता ॥ 3.293.24

savitrya pritaya datta savitrya hutaya hyapi
savitrityeva namasyascakrurviprastatha pita

—3.293.24

Simple meaning—The daughter was given to Ashvapati by Goddess Savitri, who was pleased by the chanting of gayatri mantra, therefore the father (Ashvapati) as well as the priests gave the name 'Savitri' to the daughter.

8.5 Savitri grew up, unsurpassed in beauty, wisdom and virtue. However, awed by her radiance, no one came forward to seek her hand. So her father sent her off to find a match for herself:

राजोवाच
पुत्रि प्रदानकालस्ते न च कश्चिद् वृणोति माम् ।
स्वयमन्विच्छ भर्तारं गुणैः सदृशमात्मनः ॥ 3.293.32

rajovaca
putri pradanakalaste na ca kascid vrinoti mam
svayamanviccha bhartaram gunaih sadrisamatmanah

—3.293.32

Simple meaning—King Ashvapati said to his daughter Savitri, "My dear, this is the right time when you should get married. However, awed by your radiance, no one has come forward to seek your hand. Therefore, you yourself have to find the suitable match (*i.e.* one who is as qualified as you are)."

प्रार्थितः पुरुषो यश्च स निवेद्यस्त्वया मम ।
विमृश्याहं प्रदास्यामि वरय त्वं यथेप्सितम् ॥ 3.293.33

prarthitah puruso yasca sa nivedyastvaya mama
vimrisyaham pradasyami varaya tvam yathepsitam

—3.293.33

Simple meaning—Ashvapati clarified to Savitri what he had in his mind, "When you have found a suitable match, tell me about that young man so that, after due consideration, I shall finalize your marriage with him. But you have to choose one whom you like."

8.6 Savitri travelled to various places and finally succeeded in finding a suitable match for herself. When she returned to her father to make the announcement, Rishi Narada also happened to be there.

सावित्र्युवाच

आसीच्छाल्वेषु धर्मात्मा क्षत्रियः पृथिवीपतिः ।
द्युमत्सेन इति ख्यातः पश्चाच्चान्धो बभूव ह ॥ 3.294.7
विनष्टचक्षुषस्तस्य बालपुत्रस्य धीमतः ।
सामीप्येन हृतं राज्यं छिद्रेऽस्मिन् पूर्ववैरिणा ॥ 3.294.8
तस्य पुत्रः पुरे जातः संवृद्धश्च तपोवने।
सत्यवाननुरूपो मे भर्तेति मनसा वृतः ॥ 3.294.10

asicchalvesu dharmatma ksatriyah prithivipatih
dyumatsena iti khyatah pascaccandho babhuva ha
—3.294.7

vinastacaksusastasya balaputrasya dhimatah
samipyena hritam rajyam chidresmin purvavairina
—3.294.8

tasya putrah pure jatah samvriddhasca tapovane
satyavananurupo me bharteti manasa vritah
—3.294.10

Simple meaning—Savitri made the announcement, "I have identified Satyavan as my husband-to-be. His father Dyumatsen used to be a king, but suddenly he became blind, so a neighboring ruler deprived Dyumatsen of his kingdom. He now lives in the woods, with his wife and son (*i.e.* Satyavan). Although Satyavan was born in a city, he has grown up in the righteous atmosphere of the woods."

8.7 Ashvapati asked Rishi Narada (who could read the future also) as to how suitable a match Satyavan is. The Rishi then listed the various qualities of Satyavan.

नारद उवाच

सत्यं वदत्यस्य पिता सत्यं माता प्रभाषते ।
तथास्य ब्राह्मणाश्चक्रुर्नामैतत् सत्यवानिति ॥ 3.294.12

narada uvaca
satyam vadatyasya pita satyam mata prabhasate
tathasya brahmanascakrurnamaitat satyavaniti
—3.294.12

Simple meaning—Rishi Narada said, "Satyavan's parents have always been devoted to truth, so they gave to their son, the name 'Satyavan' (which means 'truthful')."

स दान्तः स मृदुः शूरः स सत्यः संयतेन्द्रियः ।
स मैत्रः सोऽनसूयश्च स ह्रीमान् द्युतिमांश्च सः ॥ 3.294.19
नित्यशश्चार्जवं तस्मिन् स्थितिस्तस्यैव च ध्रुवा
संक्षेपतस्तपोवृद्धैः शीलवृद्धैश्च कथ्यते ॥ 3.294.20

sa dantah sa mriduh surah sa satyah samyatendriyah
sa maitrah sonasuyasca sa hriman dyutimamsca sah
—3.294.19

nityasascarjavam tasmin sthitistasyaiva ca dhruva
sanksepatastapovriddhaih silavriddhaisca kathyate
—3.294.20

Simple meaning—"Satyavan is great in self-discipline, he is brave but mild, truthful as well as avoiding extremes. He is friendly towards all, he does not find faults of others, he has a great personality but he does not show it off. He has been brought up in the woods sanctified by Rishis-they admire him as having a gentle, calm and stable personality."

8.8 अश्वपतिरुवाच
गुणैरुपेतं सर्वैस्तं भगवन् प्रब्रवीषि मे ।
दोषानप्यस्य मे ब्रूहि यदि सन्तीह केचन ॥ 3.294.21

asvapatiruvaca
gunairupetam sarvaistam bhagavan prabravisi me
dosanapsyasya me bruhi yadi santiha kecana
—3.294.21

Simple meaning—Ashvapati said to Rishi Narada, "You have narrated Satyavan's qualities and I am happy to hear about them. But please tell me if Satyavan has any shortcoming too."

8.9 नारद उवाच

एको दोषोऽस्ति नान्योऽस्य सोऽद्यप्रभृति सत्यवान् ।
संवत्सरेण क्षीणायुर्देहन्यासं करिष्यति ॥ 3.294.23

narada uvaca

eko dososti nanyosya sodyaprabhriti satyavan
samvatsarena ksinayurdehanyasam karisyati
—3.294.23

Simple meaning—Narada said, "O King, I see only one problem, viz. that Satyavan's life span will come to an end after one year from today and he will give up this body."

8.10 राजोवाच

एहि सावित्रि गच्छस्व अन्यं वरय शोभने ।
तस्य दोषो महानेको गुणानाक्रम्य च स्थितः ॥ 3.294.24

rajovaca

ehi savitri gacchasva anyam varaya sobhane
tasya doso mahaneko gunanakramya ca sthitah
—3.294.24

Simple meaning—King Ashvapati said to his daughter Savitri, "My dear, I am so nervous after listening to the Rishi's words. I suggest that you travel once more and choose someone else, other than Satyavan because his life span will come to an end after one year."

8.11 सावित्र्युवाच

सकृदंशो निपतति सकृत् कन्या प्रदीयते ।
सकृदाह ददानीति त्रीण्येतानि सकृत् सकृत् ॥ 3.294.26
दीर्घायुरथवाल्पायुः सगुणो निर्गुणोऽपि वा ।
सकृद् वृतो मया भर्ता न द्वितीयं वृणोम्यहम् ॥ 3.294.27

savitryuvaca

sakridamso nipatati sakrit kanya pradiyate
sakridaha dadaniti trinyetani sakrit sakrit
—3.294.26

dirghayurathavalpayuh saguno nirgunopi va
sakrid vrito maya bharta na dvitiyam vrinomyaham
—3.294.27

Simple meaning—However, Savitri's firm determination was not shaken, and she announced again, "My respected father, please excuse me for not changing my earlier decision. I believe in the old saying that there are three things in life which take place only once (*i.e.* decisions relating to them are made only once) and these three things are-division of property among brothers, giving away of one's daughter in marriage, and use of the words 'I give' while making a donation. Moving on from a general statement to my particular situation, I have already announced that I have identified Satyavan as my husband-to-be. That decision of mine is final, and is not subject to change, whether he will have a long life or a short life, and whether he has qualities or does not have qualities-under no circumstances am I going to choose another husband."

8.12 Ashvapati travelled with Savitri to the woods where Satyavan and his parents lived, to perform a simple marriage ceremony. Satyavan's father, Dyumatsen, while welcoming Savitri as his daughter-in-law, wondered how she will adjust to life in the woods. However, Savitri's enthusiastic acceptance of her new role set every one's mind at rest.

गते पितरि सर्वाणि संन्यस्याभरणानि सा ।
जगृहे वल्कलान्येव वस्त्रं काषायमेव च ॥ 3.295.18

gate pitari sarvani samnyasyabharanani sa
jagrihe valkalanyeva vastram kasayameva ca
—3.295.18

Simple meaning—After the marriage ceremony (of Savitri and Satyavan), Ashvapati returned to his kingdom. When her father had departed, Savitri put off all her ornaments, and clad herself in barks and red-coloured clothes appropriate to life in the woods.

8.13 परिचारैर्गुणैश्चैव प्रश्रयेण दमेन च ।
सर्वकामक्रियाभिश्च सर्वेषां तुष्टिमादधे ॥ 3.295.19

paricarairgunaiscaiva prasrayena damena ca
sarvakamakriyabhisca sarvesam tustimadadhe
—*3.295.19*

Simple meaning—Savitri earned everyone's pleasure and appreciation, because of her selfless service, good qualities, tenderness, self-denial, and performance of acts suited to everyone's needs and desires.

श्वश्रूं शरीरसत्कारैः सर्वैराच्छादनादिभिः ।
श्वशुरं देवसत्कारैर्वाचः संयमनेन च ॥ 3.295.20
svasrum sarirasatkaraih sarvairacchadanadibhih
svasuram devasatkarairvacah samyamanena ca
—*3.295.20*

Simple meaning—Savitri gratified her mother-in-law by attending to her specific needs and by offering her suitable clothes and ornaments. Similary, she earned the blessings of her father-in-law by respecting him and by using words that reflected her self-discipline.

तथैव प्रियवादेन नैपुणेन शमेन च ।
रहश्चैवोपचारेण भर्तारं पर्यतोषयत् ॥ 3.295.21
tathaiva priyavadena naipunena samena ca
rahascaivopacarena bhartaram paryatosayat
—*3.295.21*

Simple meaning—Savitri pleased her husband by her sweet words, her skill in every kind of work, the evenness of her temper, and by spending adequate time with him in private.

8.14 एवं तत्राश्रमे तेषां तदा निवसतां सताम् ।
कालस्तपस्यतां कश्चिदपाक्रामत भारत ॥ 3.295.22
evam tatrasrame tesam tada nivasatam satam
kalastapasyatam kascidapakramata bharata
—*3.295.22*

Simple meaning—Rishi Markandeya said to Yudhisthira, "O descendant of Bharata, encouraged by the sweet behaviour of Savitri, the family intensified their spiritual practices and spent their time in that nice environment (where other pious dwellers of the woods also lived.)"

सावित्र्या ग्लायमानायास्तिष्ठन्त्यास्तु दिवानिशम् ।
नारदेन यदुक्तं तद् वाक्यं मनसि वर्तते ॥ 3.295.23

savitrya glayamanayastisthantyastu divanisam
naradena yaduktam tad vakyam manasi vartate

—3.295.23

Simple meaning—Rishi Markandeya added, "Although, outwardly, everything appeared to be moving on nicely, there was no peace in the mind of Savitri, because she was the only one in that group who knew what Rishi Narada had predicted about Satyavan's life—she recalled those words day and night and sorrow filled her heart."

8.15 Finally, the fateful day arrived when, according to Rishi Narada's forecast, Satyavan's life was destined to come to an end. Savitri did not want her husband to go alone to the wood-cutting section of the forest on that day, so she got permission from her parents-in-law and accompanied Satyavan.

उभाभ्यामभ्यनुज्ञाता सा जगाम यशस्विनी ।
सह भर्त्रा हसन्तीव हृदयेन विदूयता ॥ 3.296.29

ubhabhyamabhyanujnata sa jagama yasasvini
saha bhartra hasantiva hridayena viduyata

—3.296.29

Simple meaning—Savitri obtained permission from both (*i.e.* her mother-in-law and father-in-law) to go with Satyavan to the woods on that day (without telling anyone why that day was so special). Outwardly, she was smiling as she walked with her husband, but she was extremely sad at heart (as if burning with fire of grief).

अनुव्रजन्ती भर्तारं जगाम मृदुगामिनी ।
द्विधेव हृदयं कृत्वा तं च कालमवेक्षती ॥ 3.296.33

anuvrajanti bhartaram jagama mridugamini
dvidheva hridayam kritva tam ca kalamaveksati

—3.296.33

Simple meaning—Rishi Markandeya draws attention to Savitri's capability to face the approaching crisis-it was as if she divided her heart into two parts, using one part to walk with Satyavan (without giving him any hint of what she was afraid of), and using the other part to wait for the arrival of the messenger of death.

8.16 Satyavan suddenly felt pain all over his body, and unable to walk or stand any longer, he lay down on the ground, as if fast asleep.

सत्यवानुवाच
व्यायामेन ममानेन जाता शिरसि वेदना ॥ 3.297.3
अंगानि चैव सावित्रि हृदयं दूयतीव च ।
अस्वस्थमिव चात्मानं लक्षये मितभाषिणि ॥ 3.297.4

satyavanuvaca
vyayamena mamanena jata sirasi vedana
—3.297.3

angani caiva savitri hridayam duyativa ca
asvasthamiva catmanam laksaye mitabhasini
—3.297.4

Simple meaning—Satyavan said to Savitri, "O dear, it seems that the hard work involved in cutting wood has caused me headache and pain all over my body. I also have a burning sensation in my heart. In fact, I am feeling quite unwell."

शूलैरिव शिरो विद्धमिदं संलक्षयाम्यहम् ।
तत् स्वप्तुमिच्छे कल्याणि न स्थातुं शक्तिरस्ति मे ॥ 3.297.5
sulairiva siro viddhamidam samlaksayamyaham
tat svaptumicche kalyani na sthatum saktirasti me
—3.297.5

Simple meaning—Satyavan added, "O Savitri, I feel as if my head is being pierced with numerous darts. O my well-wisher, I want to sleep because I don't have any strength to stand."

8.17 Savitri noticed the presence of an extraordinary being, staring at Satyavan. Full of fear in her heart, she addressed that being.

सावित्र्युवाच

दैवतं त्वाभिजानामि वपुरेतद्ध्यमानुषम् ।
कामया ब्रूहि देवेश कस्त्वं किं च चिकीर्षसि ॥ 3.297.11

savitryuvaca
daivatam tvabhijanami vapuretaddhyamanusam
kamaya bruhi devesa kastvam kim ca cikirsasi
—3.297.11

Simple meaning—Savitri said, "O divine being, I feel you are a god because your body is different from that of human beings. May I ask you who you are and what you want to do."

8.18 यम उवाच

पतिव्रतासि सावित्रि तथैव च तपोन्विता ।
अतस्त्वामभिभाषामि विद्धि मां त्वं शुभे यमम् ॥ 3.297.12
अयं ते सत्यवान् भर्ता क्षीणायुः पार्थिवात्मजः ।
नेष्यामि तमहं बद्ध्वा विद्ध्येतन्मे चिकीर्षितम् ॥ 3.297.13

yama uvaca
pativratasi savitri tathaiva ca taponvita
atastvamabhibhasami viddhi mam tvam subhe yamam
—3.297.12

ayam te satyavan bharta ksinayuh parthivatmajah
nesyami tamaham baddhva viddhyetanme cikirsitam
—3.297.13

Simple meaning—Yama (God of Death) said, "O Savitri, I am Yama. Normally I do not talk with human beings, but you are special becasue you are a righteous woman and a devoted wife. I have come here to take life out of the body of your husband, Satyavan, because his life span has come to an end."

सावित्र्युवाच

श्रूयते भगवन् दूतास्तवागच्छन्ति मानवान् ।
नेतुं किल भवान् कस्मादागतोऽसि स्वयं प्रभो ॥ 3.297.14

savitryuvaca
sruyate bhagavan dutastavagacchanti manavan
netum kila bhavan kasmadagatosi svayam prabho
—3.297.14

Simple meaning—Savitri said, "O divine being, I was under the impression that your messengers come to the world to take life out of human beings, so I wonder why you have yourself come here today."

यम उवाच

अयं च धर्मसंयुक्तो रूपवान् गुणसागरः ।
नार्हो मत्पुरुषैर्नेतुमतोऽस्मि स्वयमागतः ॥ 3.297.16

yama uvaca

ayam ca dharmasamyukto rupavan gunasagarah
narho matpurusairnetumatosmi svayamagatah
—3.297.16

Simple meaning—Yama said, "My messengers are not competent to take life out of Satyavan (who is an extraordinary human being), therefore I have myself come here."

8.19 When Yama started going back (with Satyavan's life), Savitri followed him. She was able to do so because of the strength of her character. But Yama advised her not to follow him any longer.

यम उवाच

निवर्त गच्छ सावित्रि कुरुष्वास्यौर्ध्वदेहिकम् ।
कृतं भर्तुस्त्वयाऽनृण्यं यावद् गम्यं गतं त्वया ॥ 3.297.20

yama uvaca

nivarta gaccha savitri kurusvasyaurdhvadehikam
kritam bhartustvayanrinyam yavad gamyam gatam tvaya
—3.297.20

Simple meaning—Yama said, "O Savitri, you have followed me long enough. I advise you not to do so any longer. Rather, I suggest that you go home and perform cremation ceremony for Satyavan. That is the only item of work that remains to be done by you, to repay the debt that you owed to your husband."

8.20 सावित्र्युवाच

यत्र मे नीयते भर्ता स्वयं वा यत्र गच्छति ।
मया च तत्र गन्तव्यमेष धर्मः सनातनः ॥ 3.297.21

तपसा गुरुभक्त्या च भर्तुः स्नेहाद् व्रतेन च ।
तव चैव प्रसादेन न मे प्रतिहता गति : ॥ 3.297.22

savitryuvaca

yatra me niyate bharta svayam va yatra gacchati
maya ca tatra gantavyamesa dharmah sanatanah
—3.297.21

tapasa gurubhaktya ca bhartuh snehad vratena ca
tava caiva prasadena na me pratihata gatih
—3.297.22

Simple meaning—Savitri said to Yama, "As a follower of Sanatan (Vedic) dharma, I must go wherever my husband goes or is being taken. And I can do so because my dharma and your grace together give me unrestricted access to all places in the universe."

प्राहुः साप्तपदं मैत्रं बुधास्तत्त्वार्थदर्शिनः ।
मित्रतां च पुरस्कृत्य किंचिद् वक्ष्यामि तच्छृणु ॥ 3.297.23
prahuh saptapadam maitram budhastattvarthadarsinah
mitratam ca puraskritya kincid vaksyami tacchrinu
—3.297.23

Simple meaning—"Wise people say that by walking together "seven steps", a new friendship is established, so considering you as a friend, I want to say a few words, and I hope you will please let me do so."

स्वधर्मेणैव हि सतां मतेन
सर्वे स्म तं मार्गमनुप्रपन्नाः।
विज्ञानतो धर्ममुदाहरन्ति
तस्मात् सन्तो धर्ममाहुः प्रधानम् ॥ 3.297.24-25
svadharmenaiva hi satam matena
sarve sma tam margamanuprapannah
vijnanato dharmamudaharanti
tasmat santo dharmamahuh pradhanam
—3.297.24-25

Simple meaning—"In the opinion of wise people, the easiest way to be with God all the time, is to follow Svadharma (as taught in Bhagavad-Gita). But the practice of Svadharma has to be guided by a scientific approach, which makes it appropriate to each occasion. Such combination of Svadharma and scientific approach is the essence of dharma as taught by spiritual leaders."

8.21 यम उवाच

निवर्त तुष्टोऽस्मि तवानया गिरा
स्वराक्षरव्यंजनहेतुयुक्तया ।
वरं वृणीष्वेह विनास्य जीवितं
ददानि ते सर्वमनिन्दिते वरम् ॥ 3.297.26

yama uvaca
nivarta tustosmi tavanaya gira
svaraksaravyanjanahetuyuktaya
varam vrinisveha vinasya jivitam
dadani te sarvamanindite varam

—3.297.26

Simple meaning—Yama said to Savitri, "O faultless lady, please do not follow me any more. I am highly pleased with the way you have spoken to me-you have expressed wonderful ideas, beautifully. Ask for a boon-I shall grant you any boon other than the life of Satyavan.

8.22 सावित्र्युवाच

च्युतः स्वराज्याद् वनवासमाश्रितो
विनष्टचक्षुः श्वशुरो ममाश्रमे ।
स लब्धचक्षुर्बलवान् भवेन्नृपः
तव प्रसादाज्ज्वलनार्कसंनिभः ॥ 3.297.27

savitryuvaca
cyutah svarajyad vanavasamasrito
vinastacaksuh svasuro mamasrame
sa labdhacaksurbalavan bhavennripah
tava prasadajjvalanarkasamnibhah

—3.297.27

Simple meaning—Savitri said to Yama, "O kind-hearted god, the favour that I seek from you is for the restoration of my father-in-law's eyesight-having lost his kingdom as well as eyesight, he is leading a life of retirement in the woods. I pray that by your grace, he may get back his eye-sight and he may be strong and effulgent like the fire and sun."

8.23 यम उवाच

ददानि तेऽहं तमनिन्दिते वरं
यथा त्वयोक्तं भविता च तत् तथा।
तवाध्वना ग्लानिमिवोपलक्षये
निवर्त गच्छस्व न ते श्रमो भवेत्॥ 3.297.28

yama uvaca
dadani teham tamanindite varam
yatha tvayoktam bhavita ca tat tatha
tavadhvana glanimivopalaksaye
nivarta gacchasva na te sramo bhavet

—3.297.28

Simple meaning—Yama said to Savitri, "O faultless lady, I grant you your wish (*i.e.* your father-in-law's eye-sight). I notice that, due to the long walk, you look quite tired. I advise you to go back, to avoid getting more tired."

8.24 सावित्र्युवाच

श्रमः कुतो भर्तृसमीपतो हि मे
यतो हि भर्ता मम सा गतिर्ध्रुवा।
यतः पतिं नेष्यसि तत्र मे गतिः
सुरेश भूयश्च वचो निबोध मे॥ 3.297.29

savitryuvaca
sramah kuto bhartrisamipato hi me
yato hi bharta mama sa gatirdhruva
yatah patim nesyasi tatra me gatih
suresa bhuyasca vaco nibodha me

—3.297.29

Simple meaning—Savitri said to Yama, "How can I get tired by walking so as to be near my husband? In fact, I can't even think of giving up such a walk. Therefore, I shall keep on following you. So please do not ask me to go back. Also please listen to my views on keeping company of good people in general."

सतां सकृत्संगतमीप्सितं परं
ततः परं मित्रमिति प्रचक्षते ।
न चाफलं सत्पुरुषेण संगतं
ततः सतां सन्निवसेत् समागमे ॥ 3.297.30

satam sakritsangatamipsitam param
tatah param mitramiti pracaksate
no caphalam satpurusena sangatam
tatah satam sannivaset samagame

—3.297.30

Simple meaning—"Even a brief contact with good people is a great thing. To become a friend of good people gives unlimited happiness. Therefore, the best advice to human beings is "Live in the company of good people." "

8.25 यम उवाच

मनोऽनुकूलं बुधबुद्धिवर्धनं
त्वया यदुक्तं वचनं हिताश्रयम् ।
विना पुनः सत्यवतोऽस्य जीवितम्
वरं द्वितीयं वरयस्व भामिनि ॥ 3.297.31

yama uvaca
manonukulam budhabuddhivardhanam
tvaya yaduktam vacanam hitasrayam
vina punah satyavatosya jivitam
varam dvitiyam varayasva bhamini

—3.297.31

Simple meaning—Yama said to Savitri, "O wise lady, the statement that you have made is beneficial to all-I am pleased with this and it can enhance the wisdom of even the learned people - therefore, I shall grant you a second boon (other than Satyavan's life).

8.26 सावित्र्युवाच

हृतं पुरा मे श्वशुरस्य धीमतः
स्वमेव राज्यं लभतां स पार्थिवः ।
जह्यात् स्वधर्मं न च मे गुरुर्यथा
द्वितीयमेतद् वरयामि ते वरम् ॥ 3.297.32

savitryuvaca
hritam pura me svasurasya dhimatah
svameva rajyam labhatam sa parthivah
jahyat svadharmam na ca me gururyatha
dvitiyametad varayami te varam

—3.297.32

Simple meaning—Savitri said to Yama, "O generous God, the second favour that I seek from you is for the restoration of my father-in-law's kingdom. Although my father-in-law is wise, his kingdom was snatched away from him. I pray that by your grace, he may regain his kingdom, and that his devotion to dharma may remain steadfast for ever."

8.27 यम उवाच

स्वमेव राज्यं प्रतिपत्स्यतेऽचिरात्
न च स्वधर्मात् परिहास्यते नृपः ।
कृतेन कामेन मया नृपात्मजे
निवर्त गच्छस्व न ते श्रमो भवेत् ॥ 3.297.33

yama uvaca
svameva rajyam pratipatsyatecirat
na ca svadharmat parihasyate nripah
kritena kamena maya nripatmaje
nivarta gacchasva na te sramo bhavet

—3.297.33

Simple mening—Yama said to Savitri, "O great princess, as desired by you, your father-in-law will get back his kingdom and his devotion to Svadharma will remain steadfast for ever. Now that I have fulfilled your wishes, I advise you to go back, to avoid getting tired."

8.28 सावित्र्युवाच

प्रजास्त्वयैता नियमेन संयता
नियम्य चैता नयसे निकामया ।
ततो यमत्वं तव देव विश्रुतं
निबोध चेमां गिरमीरितां मया ॥ 3.297.34

savitryuvaca

prajastvayaita niyamena samyata
niyamya caita nayase nikamaya
tato yamatvam tava deva visrutam
nibodha cemam giramiritam maya

—3.297.34

Simple meaning—Savitri said to Yama, "O discipline-promoting God, I learnt from my parents that it is due to your guidance that all the people in the universe lead a regulated life. I hope you will let me say a few words about what I have learnt about Sanatana dharma."

अद्रोहः सर्वभूतेषु कर्मणा मनसा गिरा ।
अनुग्रहश्च दानं च सतां धर्मः सनातनः ॥ 3.297.35

adrohah sarvabhutesu karmana manasa gira
anugrahasca danam ca satam dharmah sanatanah

—3.297.35

Simple meaning—"The main teachings of Sanatana (Vedic) dharma are that people should support one another, by thought, word and deed, and that they should share equitably, whatever they have."

एवंप्रायश्च लोकोऽयं मनुष्याः शक्तिपेशलाः ।
सन्तस्त्वेवाप्यमित्रेषु दयां प्राप्तेषु कुर्वते ॥ 3.297.36

evamprayasca lokoyam manusyah saktipesalah
santastvevapyamitresu dayam praptesu kurvate

—3.297.36

Simple meaning—"Mutual support is essential because common people by themselves would be unable to live happily. Best people are those who show compassion even towards enemies if they seek protection."

8.29 यम उवाच

पिपासितस्येव भवेद् यथा पयः
तथा त्वया वाक्यमिदं समीरितम् ।
विना पुनः सत्यवतोऽस्य जीवितं
वरं वृणीष्वेह शुभे यदिच्छसि ॥ 3.297.37

yama uvaca
pipasitasyeva bhaved yatha payah
tatha tvaya vakyamidam samiritam
vina punah satyavatosya jivitam
varam vrinisveha subhe yadicchasi

—3.297.37

Simple meaning—Yama said to Savitri, "O good lady, as water gives relief to the thirsty soul, so do I feel pleasure by listening to your wise statement. Therefore, I shall grant you a third boon (other than Satyavan's life)—if you would like to ask for it."

8.30 सावित्र्युवाच

ममानपत्यः पृथिवीपतिः पिता
भवेत् पितुः पुत्रशतं तथौरसम् ।
कुलस्य सन्तानकरं च यद् भवेत्
तृतीयमेतद् वरयामि ते वरम् ॥ 3.297.38

savitryuvaca
mamanapatyah prithivipatih pita
bhavet pituh putrasatam tathaurasam
kulasya santanakaram ca yad bhavet
tritiyametad varayami te varam

—3.297.38

Simple meaning—Savitri said to Yama, "O merciful God, the third boon that I seek is that my parents (who have no sons) should have sons to carry forward the dharmic tradition of the family."

8.31 यम उवाच

कुलस्य सन्तानकरं सुवर्चसं
शतं सुतानां पितुरस्तु ते शुभे ।

कृतेन कामेन नराधिपात्मजे
निवर्त दूरं हि पथस्त्वमागता ॥ 3.297.39

yama uvaca
kulasya santanakaram suvarcasam
satam sutanam piturastu te subhe
kritena kamena naradhipatmaje
nivarta duram hi pathastvamagata

—3.297.39

Simple meaning—Yama said to Savitri, "O good princess, I will have your wish accomplished, viz. that your parents will have sons to carry forward the great family tradition. Now that I have fulfilled three wishes of yours, I advise that you go back-you have walked such a long distance."

8.32 सावित्र्युवाच

न दूरमेतन्मम भर्तृसंनिधौ
मनो हि मे दूरतरं प्रधावति ।
अथ व्रजन्नेव गिरं समुद्यतां
मयोच्यमानां श्रणु भूय एव च ॥ 3.297.40

savitryuvaca
na durametanmama bhartrisamnidhau
mano hi me durataram pradhavati
atha vrajanneva giram samudyatam
mayocyamanam srinu bhuya eva ca

—3.297.40

Simple meaning—Savitri said to Yama, "O compassionate God, you feel that I have walked too long, but since I have walked so as to be near my husband, the distance walked has not bothered me. In fact, my mind has travelled even further. Without slowing down, I would like to say a few words, and I hope you will listen to them."

विवस्वतस्त्वं तनयः प्रतापवान्
ततो हि वैवस्वत उच्यसे बुधैः ।
समेन धर्मेण चरन्ति ताः प्रजाः
ततस्तवेहेश्वर धर्मराजता ॥ 3.297.41

vivasvatastvam tanayah pratapavan
tato hi vaivasvata ucyase budhaih
samena dharmena caranti tah prajah
tatastavehesvara dharmarajata

—3.297.41

Simple meaning—"O generous God, I learnt from my parents that you are the mighty son of the sun-god, that you are in charge of preserving people's observance of dharma, and that you are setting the example of perfect observance of dharma while dealing with all the human beings of the universe."

आत्मन्यपि न विश्वासस्तथा भवति सत्सु वः ।
तस्मात् सत्सु विशेषेण सर्वः प्रणयमिच्छति ॥ 3.297.42

atmanyapi na visvasastatha bhavati satsu vah
tasmat satsu visesena sarvah pranayamicchati

—3.297.42

Simple meaning—"To understand the observance of dharma, in day-to-day life, human beings receive guidance from righteous people or saints. That is why they have a worshipful attitude towards saints."

सौहृदात् सर्वभूतानां विश्वासो नाम जायते ।
तस्मात् सत्सु विशेषेण विश्वासं कुरुते जनः ॥ 3.297.43

sauhridat sarvabhutanam visvaso nama jayate
tasmat satsu visesena visvasam kurute janah

—3.297.43

Simple meaning—"Righteous people or saints provide guidance to human beings, in a spirit of friendliness, and because of that, they earn the confidence of all."

8.33 यम उवाच

उदाहृतं ते वचनं यदंगने
शुभे न तादृक् त्वदृते श्रुतं मया ।
अनेन तुष्टोऽस्मि विनास्य जीवितं
वरं चतुर्थं वरयस्व गच्छ च ॥ 3.297.44

yama uvaca

udahritam te vacanam yadangane
subhe na tadrik tvadrite srutam maya
anena tustosmi vinasya jivitam
varam caturtham varayasva gaccha ca

—3.297.44

Simple meaning—Yama said to Savitri, "O exemplary lady, I have never heard from any one else such a nice statement as you have spoken. I am so pleased with you that I shall grant you a fourth boon (other than Satyavan's life)-and thereafter you should go back."

8.34 सावित्र्युवाच

ममात्मजं सत्यवतस्तथौरसं
भवेदुभाभ्यामिह यत् कुलोद्वहम् ।
शतं सुतानां बलवीर्यशालिनां
इदं चतुर्थं वरयामि ते वरम् ॥ 3.297.45

savitryuvaca

mamatmajam satyavatastathaurasam
bhavedubhabhyamiha yat kulodvaham
satam sutanam balaviryasalinam
idam caturtham varayami te varam

—3.297.45

Simple meaning—Savitri said to Yama, "O boon-granting god, the fourth boon that I look forward to receiving from you is, that I and Satyavan may have sons, possessed of strength and prowess and capable of carrying forward the dharmic tradition of this family."

8.35 यम उवाच

शतं सुतानां बलवीर्यशालिनां
भविष्यति प्रीतिकरं तवाबले ।
परिश्रमस्ते न भवेन्नृपात्मजे
निवर्त दूरं हि पथस्त्वमागता ॥ 3.297.46

yama uvaca
satam sutanam balaviryasalinam
bhavisyati pritikaram tavabale
parisramaste na bhavennripatmaje
nivarta duram hi pathastvamagata

—3.297.46

Simple meaning—Yama said to Savitri, "O patient lady, I grant you this boon and you will have sons, possessed of strength and prowess, and a source of great delight to you. O princess, I now ask you to go back—you have already come too far and must be feeling tired."

8.36 Savitri pleaded that walking behind her husband did not cause any fatigue. She was grateful to have the opportunity of talking with a generous God whose mission was to help everyone and thus to bear the burden of the world.

सावित्र्युवाच

सन्तः परार्थं कुर्वाणा
नावेक्षन्ति परस्परम् ॥ 3.297.49
सन्तो भूमिं तपसा धारयन्ति ॥ 3.297.48

savitryuvaca
santah parartham kurvana
naveksanti parasparam

—3.297.49

santo bhumim tapsa dharayanti

—3.297.48

Simple meaning—Savitri said to Yama, "O generous God, you have inspired good persons to do good to others without expecting any benefit for themselves in return. Through this type of spiritual practice, they are able to sustain the world."

8.37 यम उवाच

यथा यथा भाषसि धर्मसंहितं
मनोऽनुकूलं सुपदं महार्थवत् ।

तथा तथा मे त्वयि भक्तिरुत्तमा
वरं वृणीष्वाप्रतिमं पतिव्रते ॥ 3.297.51

yama uvaca
yatha yatha bhasasi dharmasamhitam
manonukulam supadam maharthavat
tatha tatha me tvayi bhaktiruttama
varam vrinisvapratimam pativrate

—3.297.51

Simple meaning—Yama said to Savitri, "O great lady spiritually devoted to husband, the more I hear your statements that contain the nectar of dharma, expressed in such sweet and appealing terms, the more affection I feel towards you. Therefore, I shall grant you a special, fifth boon."

8.38 सावित्र्युवाच

न तेऽपवर्गः सुकृताद् विनाकृतः
तथा यथान्येषु वरेषु मानद ।
वरं वृणे जीवतु सत्यवानयं
यथा मृता ह्येवमहं पतिं विना ॥ 3.297.52

savitryuvaca
na tepavargah sukritad vinakritah
tatha yathanyesu varesu manada
varam vrine jivatu satyavanayam
yatha mrita hyevamaham patim vina

—3.297.52

Simple meaning—Savitri said to Yama, "O bestower of honours, the fourth boon that you granted to me was itself a special boon, because it can be fulfilled only when I live with my husband. In fact, without my husband, I am like a dead person. Therefore, the special boon that I now specifically seek is that Satyavan may come to life again."

8.39 Yama accepted Savitri's plea, and released Satyavan's life. Savitri then returned and found that her husband was alive. Satyavan himself felt as if he woke up from a long sleep. Then both of them walked back home to see the mother and the father (the latter's eye-sight having been restored by Yama). Everyone felt happy and amazed when they heard from Savitri the full story of her encounter with Yama.

8.40 Vidyut Aklujkar has summarized the virtues of Savitri as a truly great woman who faced the most serious crisis triumphantly:

"When Satyavan dies, Savitri does not lament. Hers is only a calm, resolute confrontation with Death. She has the strength of character that is a natural outcome of a life of righteous observances, and although she is neither impolite nor aggressive, she never gives up. As a true Karmayogin, she accepts whatever is offered to her and perseveres in the quest for more. In the end, when she returns, she has her mission fulfilled and has earned a perennial place in the list of great women." [1]

Chapter 9

How Yudhisthira Brought his Brothers Back to Life

9.1 A crisis, caused by the apparent death of his four brothers, confronted Yudhisthira when he was about to complete twelve years of stay in the forest. But he did not lose heart. When he went to the place where his brothers lay lifeless, he entered into a dialogue with Yaksa (a supernatural being). This dialogue is one of the most important sections of the Mahabharata. Yaksa turned out to be the Lord of Dharma who wanted to test whether Yudhisthira could give appropriate answers to more than a hundred questions on various aspects of dharma. Yudhisthira came out successful in the test, and the incident that appeared to bring disaster to the Pandavas had a happy ending, because Yaksa put life back in the four brothers of Yudhisthira. We present here the Yaksa-Yudhisthira dialogue in full, because that holds the key to Yudhisthira's success in facing the crisis situation.

9.2 According to B. A. Van Nooten, "Yaksas are originally spirits of trees and of bodies of water that are locally deified and later became identified with a class of Gods of the Great Tradition. A Yaksa has monstrous eyes, a great body, is as high as a palm tree, resembling the blazing sun, irresistible, looking like a mountain. Often they are benevolent and together with the Gandharvas form the retinue of the God of Wealth, Kubera." [1]

9.3 The setting for the dialogue between Yaksa and Yudhisthira is provided by a deer who ran extremely fast and carried away with itself, as if by chance, a brahmin's fire-making sticks. The brahmin requested the Pandavas to get those sticks back from the deer, to enable him to perform his yajna. The Pandavas agreed to help but the deer ran too fast and then became invisible. Losing sight of the deer, the Pandavas, feeling tired, disappointed and thirsty, approached a banyan tree and sat down in its shade. Yudhisthira asked Nakula (one of the younger brothers) to climb the tree and look around, in a desperate attempt to find some water in that inhospitable surrounding. Nakula was able to spot a lake inhabited by cranes. However, as soon as Nakula stooped down to drink the water of the lake, he heard a voice from the sky, which was Yaksa's warning.

यक्ष उवाच
मा तात साहसं कार्षीर्मम पूर्वपरिग्रहः ।
प्रश्नानुक्त्वा तु माद्रेय ततः पिब हरस्व च ॥ 3.312.12

yaksa uvaca
ma tata sahasam karsirmama purvaparigrahah
prasnanuktva tu madreya tatah piba harasva ca
—3.312.12

Simple meaning—Yaksa said to Nakula, "Do not commit the rash act of drinking water from this lake which has already been taken by me under my control. First answer my questions and then you may drink this water and also take away as much water as you want."

However, Nakula ignored this warning and drank some water because he was extremely thirsty. Then, as if punished by Yaksa for the disregard shown to his warning, Nakula dropped down dead. When Nakula did not return with water, Yudhisthira asked the other three brothers to go, one after the other, but they all met with the same fate. Finally Yudhisthira went himself and his long conversation with Yaksa began.

9.4 After a preliminary exchange of words, Yaksa introduced himself, and in reply thereto, Yudhisthira expressed his willingness to answer all the questions according to his intellectual capacity.

युधिष्ठिर उवाच

न चाहं कामये यक्ष तव पूर्वपरिग्रहम् ।
कामं नैतत् प्रशंसन्ति सन्तो हि पुरुषाः सदा ॥ 3.313.43
यदात्मना स्वमात्मानं प्रशंसे पुरुषर्षभ ।
यथाप्रज्ञं तु ते प्रश्नान् प्रतिवक्ष्यामि पृच्छ माम् ॥ 3.313.44

yudhisthira uvaca
na caham kamaye yaksa tava purvaparigraham
kamam naitat prasamsanti santo hi purusah sada
—3.313.43
yadatmana svamatmanam prasamse purusarsabha
yathaprajnam tu te prasan prativaksyami priccha mam
—3.313.44

Simple meaning—Yudhisthira said to Yaksa, "I do not want anything which is already under your control. I also do not want to praise myself—in fact, self-praise is not approved by good people. Since you want to put questions to me, please go ahead—I shall answer all your questions according to my intellectual capacity."

9.5 In all, Yaksha put one hundred and twenty four questions—these were put in a quick sequence and most of them were asked in groups of four at a time.

यक्ष उवाच

किं स्विदादित्यमुन्नयति के च तस्याभितश्चराः ।
कश्चैनमस्तं नयति कस्मिंश्च प्रतितिष्ठति ॥ 3.313.45

yaksa uvaca
kim svidadityamunnayati ke ca tasyabhitascarah
kascainamastam nayati kasmimsca pratitisthati
—3.313.45

Simple meaning—Yaksa asked, "What is it that makes the sun rise? Who keeps him company? Who causes him to set? And in whom is he established?"

युधिष्ठिर उवाच
ब्रह्मादित्यमुन्नयति देवास्तस्याभितश्चरा : ।
धर्मश्चास्तं नयति च सत्ये च प्रतितिष्ठति ॥ 3.313.46

yudhisthira uvaca
brahmadityamunnayati devastasyabhitascarah
dharmascastam nayati ca satye ca pratitisthati
—3.313.46

Simple meaning—Yudhisthira replied, "Brahman makes the sun rise, Gods keep him company, dharma causes him to set, and he is established in truth."

9.6 यक्ष उवाच
केनस्विच्छ्रोत्रियो भवति केनस्विद् विन्दते महत् ।
केनस्विद् द्वितीयवान् भवति राजन् केन च बुद्धिमान् ॥ 3.313.47

yaksa uvaca
kenasvicchrotriyo bhavati kenasvid vindate mahat
kenasvid dvitiyavan bhavati rajan kena ca buddhiman
—3.313.47

Simple meaning—Yaksa asked, "By what does one become learned? By what does one attain what is great? How can one have a second person's company? How can one acquire the right intellect?"

युधिष्ठिर उवाच
श्रुतेन श्रोत्रियो भवति तपसा विन्दते महत् ।
धृत्या द्वितीयवान् भवति बुद्धिमान् वृद्धसेवया ॥ 3.313.48

yudhisthira uvaca
srutena srotriyo bhavati tapasa vindate mahat
dhritya dvitiyavan bhavati buddhiman vriddhasevaya
—3.313.48

Simple meaning—Yudhisthira replied, "It is by the study of Vedas and Upanisads that a person becomes learned, it is by self-discipline that one acquires what is great, it is by patience that a person can have a second person's company, and it is by serving old people that one acquires the right intellect."

9.7 यक्ष उवाच

किं ब्राह्मणानां देवत्वं कश्च धर्मः सतामिव ।
कश्चैषां मानुषो भावः किमेषामसतामिव ॥ 3.313.49

yaksa uvaca
kim brahmananam devatvam kasca dharmah satamiva
kascaisam manuso bhavah kimesamasatamiva
—3.313.49

Simple meaning—Yaksa asked, "What constitutes the divinity of the brahmins, what is their dharma like that of good people, what is their human attribute, and what practice of theirs is like that of unrighteous people?"

युधिष्ठिर उवाच

स्वाध्याय एषां देवत्वं तप एषां सतामिव ।
मरणं मानुषो भावः परिवादोऽसतामिव ॥ 3.313.50

yudhisthira uvaca
svadhyaya esam devatvam tapa esam satamiva
maranam manuso bhavah parivadosatamiva
—3.313.50

Simple meaning—Yudhisthira replied, "Study of scriptures constitutes their divinity, their self-discipline constitutes dharma like that of good people, their liability to death is their human attribute, and to speak ill of others is a practice like that of unrighteous people."

9.8 यक्ष उवाच

किं क्षत्रियाणां देवत्वं कश्च धर्मः सतामिव ।
कश्चैषां मानुषो भावः किमेषामसतामिव ॥ 3.313.51

yaksa uvaca
kim ksatriyanam devatvam kasca dharmah satamiva
kascaisam manuso bhavah kimesamasatamiva
—3.313.51

Simple meaning—Yaksa asked, "What constitutes the divinity of the Ksatriyas, what is their dharma like that of good people, what is their human attribute, and what practice of theirs is like that of unrighteous people?"

युधिष्ठिर उवाच
इष्वस्त्रमेषां देवत्वं यज्ञ एषां सतामिव ।
भयं वै मानुषो भावः परित्यागोऽसतामिव ॥ 3.313.52

yudhisthira uvaca
isvastramesam devatvam yajna esam satamiva
bhayam vai manuso bhavah parityagosatamiva
—3.313.52

Simple meaning—Yudhisthira replied, "Arrows and weapons constitute their divinity, their yajna constitutes dharma like that of good people, their liability to fear is their human attribute, and refusal of protection to those who seek their help is a practice like that of unrighteous people."

9.9 यक्ष उवाच
किमेकं यज्ञियं साम किमेकं यज्ञियं यजुः ।
का चैषां वृणुते यज्ञं कां यज्ञो नातिवर्तते ॥ 3.313.53

yaksa uvaca
kimekam yajniyam sama kimekam yajniyam yajuh
ka caisam vrinute yajnam kam yajno nativartate
—3.313.53

Simple meaning—Yaksa asked, "What is that which constitutes the equivalent of Sama-Veda in a spiritual sacrifice, what is the equivalent of Yajur-Veda, what is the equivalent of Rig-Veda, and what is that which a spiritual sacrifice cannot do without?"

युधिष्ठिर उवाच
प्राणो वै यज्ञियं साम मनो वै यज्ञियं यजुः ।
ऋगेका वृणुते यज्ञं तां यज्ञो नातिवर्तते ॥ 3.313.54

yudhisthira uvaca
prano vai yajniyam sama mano vai yajniyam yajuh
rigeka vrinute yajnam tam yajno nativartate
—3.313.54

Simple meaning—Yudhisthira replied, "Life is the equivalent of Sama-Veda in a spiritual sacrifice, mind is the equivalent of Yajur-Veda, prayerfulness is the equivalent of Rig-Veda, and it is prayerfulness alone which a spiritual sacrifice cannot do without."

9.10 यक्ष उवाच

किंस्विदावपतां श्रेष्ठं किंस्विन्निवपतां वरम् ।

किंस्वित् प्रतिष्ठमानानां किंस्वित् प्रसवतां वरम् ॥ 3.313.55

yaksa uvaca

kimsvidavapatam srestham kimsvinnivapatam varam

kimsvit pratisthamananam kimsvit prasavatam varam

—3.313.55

Simple meaning—Yaksa asked, "What is most important to those who want to prepare land for cultivation, what is most important to those who want to sow, what is most important to those who are prosperous, and what is most important to those who bring forth children?"

युधिष्ठिर उवाच

वर्षमावपतां श्रेष्ठं बीजं निवपतां वरम् ।

गावः प्रतिष्ठमानानां पुत्रः प्रसवतां वरः ॥ 3.313.56

yudhisthira uvaca

varsamavapatam srestham bijam nivasatam varam

gavah pratisthamananam putrah prasavatam varah

—3.313.56

Simple meaning—Yudhisthira replied, "Rain is most important to those who want to prepare land for cultivation, seed is most important to those who want to sow, cows are most important to those who are prosperous, and a son is most important to those who bring forth children."

9.11 यक्ष उवाच

इंद्रियार्थाननुभवन् बुद्धिमांल्लोकपूजितः ।

सम्मतः सर्वभूतानामुच्छ्वसन् को न जीवति ॥ 3.313.57

yaksa uvaca

indriyarthananubhavan buddhimamllokapujitah

sammatah sarvabhutanamucchvasan ko na jivati

—3.313.57

Simple meaning—Yaksa asked, "What person, in-spite of enjoying all the objects of the senses, endued with intelligence, regarded by the world and liked by all the beings, though breathing, is still not really alive?"

युधिष्ठिर उवाच

देवतातिथिभृत्यानां पितृणामात्मनश्च यः ।
न निर्वपति पंचानामुच्छ्वसन् न स जीवति ॥ 3.313.58

yudhisthira uvaca
devatatithibhrityanam pitrinamatmanasca yah
na nirvapati pancanamucchvasan na sa jivati
—3.313.58

Simple meaning—Yudhisthira replied, "That person who does not offer due shares to gods, guests, dependents, ancestors, and Atman (*i.e.* spiritual needs of one's own self), though breathing, is still not really alive."

9.12 यक्ष उवाच

किंस्विद् गुरुतरं भूमेः किंस्विदुच्चतरं च खात् ।
किंस्विच्छीघ्रतरं वायोः किंस्विद् बहुतरं तृणात् ॥ 3.313.59

yaksa uvaca
kimsvid gurutaram bhumeh kimsviduccataram ca khat
kimsvicchighrataram vayoh kimsvid bahutaram trinat
—3.313.59

Simple meaning—Yaksa asked, "What is weightier than the earth itself, what is higher than the heavens, what is faster than the wind, and what is more numerous than grass?"

युधिष्ठिर उवाच

माता गुरुतरा भूमेः खात् पितोच्चतरस्तथा ।
मनः शीघ्रतरं वाताच्चिन्ता बहुतरी तृणात् ॥ 3.313.60

yudhisthira uvaca
mata gurutara bhumeh khat pitoccatarastatha
manah sighrataram vataccinta bahutari trinat
—3.313.60

Simple meaning—Yudhisthira replied, "The mother is weightier than the earth, the father is higher than the heavens, mind is faster than the wind, and our thoughts are more numerous than grass."

9.13 यक्ष उवाच

किंस्वित् सुप्तं न निमिषति किंस्विज्जातं न चोपति ।
कस्यस्विद्धृदयं नास्ति किंस्विद् वेगेन वर्धते ॥ 3.313.61

yaksa uvaca
kimsvit suptam na nimisati kimsvijjatam na copati
kasyasviddhridayam nasti kimsvid vegena vardhate
—3.313.61

Simple meaning—Yaksa asked, "What is that which does not close its eyes while asleep, what is that which does not move after birth, what is that which is without heart, and what is that which swells with its own impetus?"

युधिष्ठिर उवाच

मत्स्यः सुप्तो न निमिषत्यण्डं जातं न चोपति ।
अश्मनो हृदयं नास्ति नदी वेगेन वर्धते ॥ 3.313.62

yudhisthira uvaca
matsyah supto na nimisatyandam jatam na copati
asmano hridayam nasti nadi vegena vardhate
—3.313.62

Simple meaning—Yudhisthira replied, "A fish does not close its eyes while asleep, an egg does not move after birth, a stone is without heart, and a river swells with its own impetus."

9.14 यक्ष उवाच

किंस्वित् प्रवसतो मित्रं किंस्विन्मित्रं गृहे सतः ।
आतुरस्य च किं मित्रं किंस्विन्मित्रं मरिष्यत : ॥ 3.313.63

yaksa uvaca
kimsvit pravasato mitram kimsvinmitram grihe satah
aturasya ca kim mitram kimsvinmitram marisyatah
—3.313.63

Simple meaning—Yaksa asked, "Who is the friend of one travelling far away from home, who is the friend of one living in the home, who is the friend of a sick person, and who is the friend of one about to die?"

युधिष्ठिर उवाच
सार्थः प्रवसतो मित्रं भार्या मित्रं गृहे सतः ।
आतुरस्य भिषङ्मित्रं दानं मित्रं मरिष्यतः ॥ 3.313.64

yudhisthira uvaca
sarthah pravasato mitram bharya mitram grihe satah
aturasya bhisanmitram danam mitram marisyatah
—3.313.64

Simple meaning—Yudhisthira replied, "The friend of one travelling far away from home is his companion, the friend of one living in the home is his wife, a doctor is the friend of a sick person, and charity is the friend of one about to die."

9.15 यक्ष उवाच
कोऽतिथिः सर्वभूतानां किंस्विद् धर्मं सनातनम् ।
अमृतं किंस्विद् राजेन्द्र किंस्वित् सर्वमिदं जगत् ॥ 3.313.65

yaksa uvaca
kotithih sarvabhutanam kimsvid dharmam sanatanam
amritam kimsvid rajendra kimsvit sarvamidam jagat
—3.313.65

Simple meaning—Yaksa asked, "Who is the guest of all beings, what is the dharma that has no specific beginning, what is nectar, and what constitutes this entire universe?"

युधिष्ठिर उवाच
अतिथिः सर्वभूतानामग्निः सोमो गवामृतम् ।
सनातनोऽमृतो धर्मो वायुः सर्वमिदं जगत् ॥ 3.313.66

yudhisthira uvaca
atithih sarvabhutanamagnih somo gavamritam
sanatanomrito dharmo vayuh sarvamidam jagat
—3.313.66

Simple meaning—Yudhisthira replied, "Agni (*i.e.* god of fire) is the guest of all beings, dharma based on spiritual principles has no specific beginning, cow's milk is nectar, and this entire universe consists of air alone."

9.16 यक्ष उवाच
किंस्विदेको विचरते जातः को जायते पुनः ।
किंस्विद्धिमस्य भैषज्यं किंस्विदावपनं महत् ॥ 3.313.67

yaksa uvaca
kimsvideko vicarate jatah ko jayate punah
kimsviddhimasya bhaisajyam kimsvidavapanam mahat
—3.313.67

Simple meaning—Yaksa asked, "Who travels alone, who is born again and again, what is the remedy against cold, and what is the largest ksetra (field)?"

युधिष्ठिर उवाच
सूर्य एको विचरते चन्द्रमा जायते पुनः ।
अग्निर्हिमस्य भैषज्यं भूमिरावपनं महत् ॥ 3.313.68

yudhisthira uvaca
surya eko vicarate candrama jayate punah
agnirhimasya bhaisajyam bhumiravapanam mahat
—3.313.68

Simple meaning—Yudhisthira replied, "The sun travels alone, the moon is born again and again, fire is the remedy against cold, and the earth is the largest ksetra (field)."

9.16 यक्ष उवाच
किंस्विदेकपदं धर्म्यं किंस्विदेकपदं यशः ।
किंस्विदेकपदं स्वर्ग्यं किंस्विदेकपदं सुखम् ॥ 3.313.69

yaksa uvaca
kimsvidekapadam dharmyam kimsvidekapadam yasah
kimsvidekapadam svargyam kimsvidekapadam sukham
—3.313.69

Simple meaning—Yaksa asked, "What is one main support of dharma, what is one main support of fame, what is one main support of heaven, and what is one main support of happiness?"

युधिष्ठिर उवाच
दाक्ष्यमेकपदं धर्म्यं दानमेकपदं यशः ।
सत्यमेकपदं स्वर्ग्यं शीलमेकपदं सुखम् ॥ 3.313.70

yudhisthira uvaca
daksyamekapadam dharmyam danamekapadam yasah
satyamekapadam svargyam silamekapadam sukham
—3.313.70

Simple meaning—Yudhisthira replied, "Skill in action is one main support of dharma, act of sharing is one main support of fame, truth is one main support of heaven, and good conduct is one main support of happiness."

9.18 यक्ष उवाच
किंस्विदात्मा मनुष्यस्य किंस्विद् दैवकृतः सखा ।
उपजीवनं किंस्विदस्य किंस्विदस्य परायणम् ॥ 3.313.71

yaksa uvaca
kimsvidatma manusyasya kimsvid daivakritah sakha
upajivanam kimsvidasya kimsvidasya parayanam
—3.313.71

Simple meaning—Yaksa asked, "What is the soul of man, who is the friend bestowed on man by the God, what is the chief support of human existence, and what is it that binds human beings together?"

युधिष्ठिर उवाच
पुत्र आत्मा मनुष्यस्य भार्या दैवकृतः सखा ।
उपजीवनं च पर्जन्यो दानमस्य परायणम् ॥ 3.313.72

yudhisthira uvaca
putra atma manusyasya bharya daivakritah sakha
upajivanam ca parjanyo danamasya parayanam
—3.313.72

Simple meaning—Yudhisthira replied, "A son is the soul of man, the wife is the friend bestowed on man by the God, clouds are the chief support of human existence, and acts of sharing bind human beings together."

9.19 यक्ष उवाच
धन्यानामुत्तमं किंस्विद् धनानां स्यात् किमुत्तमम् ।
लाभानामुत्तं किं स्यात् सुखानां स्यात् किमुत्तमम् ॥ 3.313.73

yaksa uvaca
dhanyanamuttamam kimsvid dhananam syat kimuttamam
labhanamuttamam kim syat sukhanam syat kimuttamam
—3.313.73

Simple meaning—Yaksa asked, "What is the best of all laudable things, what is the most valuable possession that one can have, what is the best of all gains, and what is it that gives the greatest happiness?"

युधिष्ठिर उवाच
धन्यानामुत्तमं दाक्ष्यं धनानामुत्तमं श्रुतम् ।
लाभानां श्रेय आरोग्यं सुखानां तुष्टिरुत्तमा ॥ 3.313.74

yudhisthira uvaca
dhanyanamuttamam daksyam dhananamuttamam srutam
labhanam sreya arogyam sukhanam tustiruttama
—3.313.74

Simple meaning—Yudhisthira replied, "Skill in action is the best of all laudable things, knowledge of scriptures is the most valuable possession that one can have, health is the best of all gains, and contentment gives the greatest happiness."

9.20 यक्ष उवाच
कश्च धर्मः परो लोके कश्च धर्मः सदाफलः ।
किं नयम्य न शोचन्ति कैश्च संधिर्न जीर्यते ॥ 3.313.75

yaksa uvaca
kasca dharmah paro loke kasca dharmah sadaphalah
kim nayamya na socanti kaisca sandhirna jiryate
—3.313.75

Simple meaning—Yaksa asked, "What is the highest dharma in the world, which dharmic practices do people use to obtain what they want, what is that which, if controlled, causes no regrets, and who are they whose friendship does not break?"

युधिष्ठिर उवाच
आनृशंस्यं परो धर्मस्त्रयीधर्मः सदाफलः ।
मनो यम्य न शोचन्ति संधिः सद्भिर्न जीर्यते ॥ 3.313.76

yudhisthira uvaca
anrisamsyam paro dharmastrayidharmah sadaphalah
mano yamya na socanti sandhih sadbhirna jiryate
—3.313.76

Simple meaning—Yudhisthira replied, "Absence of cruelty is the highest dharma, people use dharmic practices of the Vedas to obtain what they want, mind, if controlled, causes no regrets, and friendship with good people does not break."

9.21 यक्ष उवाच
किं नु हित्वा प्रियो भवति
किं नु हित्वा न शोचति ।
किं नु हित्वार्थवान् भवति
किं नु हित्वा सुखी भवेत् ॥ 3.313.77

yaksa uvaca
kim nu hitva priyo bhavati
kim nu hitva na socati
kim nu hitvarthavan bhavati
kim nu hitva sukhi bhavet
—3.313.77

Simple meaning—Yaksa asked, "What is that which, if given up, endears you to others, what is that which, if given up, leads to no regrets, what is that which, if given up, makes you feel wealthy, and what is that which, if given up, makes you feel happy?"

युधिष्ठिर उवाच
मानं हित्वा प्रियो भवति
क्रोधं हित्वा न शोचति ।
कामं हित्वार्थवान् भवति
लोभं हित्वा सुखी भवेत् ॥ 3.313.78

yudhisthira uvaca
manam hitva priyo bhavati
krodham hitva na socati

kamam hitvarthavan bhavati
lobham hitva sukhi bhavet

—3.313.78

Simple meaning—Yudhisthira replied, "It is arrogance which, if given up, endears you to others, it is anger which, if given up, leads to no regrets, it is selfish desires which, if given up, make you feel wealthy, and it is greed which, if given up, makes you feel happy."

9.22 यक्ष उवाच

किमर्थं ब्राह्मणे दानं किमर्थं नटनर्तके ।
किमर्थं चैव भृत्येषु किमर्थं चैव राजसु ॥ 3.313.79

yaksa uvaca

kimartham brahmane danam kimartham natanartake
kimartham caiva bhrityesu kimartham caiva rajasu

—3.313.79

Simple meaning—Yaksa asked, "What is the motive which prompts you to give money to brahmins, what is the motive which prompts you to give money to artists, what is the motive which prompts you to give money to dependents, and what is the motive which prompts you to give money to kings?"

युधिष्ठिर उवाच

धर्मार्थं ब्राह्मणे दानं यशोऽर्थं नटनर्तके ।
भृत्येषु भरणार्थं वै भयार्थं चैव राजसु ॥ 3.313.80

yudhisthira uvaca

dharmartham brahmane danam yasortham natanartake
brityesu bharanartham vai bhayartham caiva rajasu

—3.313.80

Simple meaning—Yudhisthira replied, "Dharma is the motive which prompts you to give money to brahmins, fame is the motive which prompts you to give money to artists, providing support is the motive which prompts you to give money to dependents, and obtaining relief from fear is the motive which prompts you to give money to kings."

9.23 यक्ष उवाच

केनस्विदावृतो लोकः केनस्विन्न प्रकाशते ।
केन त्यजति मित्राणि केन स्वर्गं न गच्छति ॥ 3.313.81

yaksa uvaca
kenasvidavrito lokah kenasvinna prakasate
kena tyajati mitrani kena svargam na gacchati
—3.313.81

Simple meaning—Yaksa asked, "With what is the world enveloped, why does its real nature not become known, for what are friends forsaken, and why do people fail to go to heaven?"

युधिष्ठिर उवाच

अज्ञानेनावृतो लोकस्तमसा न प्रकाशते ।
लोभात् त्यजति मित्राणि संगात् स्वर्गं न गच्छति ॥ 3.313.82

yudhisthira uvaca
ajnanenavrito lokastamasa na prakasate
lobhat tyajati mitrani sangat svargam na gacchati
—3.313.82

Simple meaning—Yudhisthira replied, "The world is enveloped with ignorance, its real nature does not become known because of unrighteousness, people forsake their friends due to greed, and they fail to go to heaven due to attachment."

9.24 यक्ष उवाच

मृतः कथं स्यात् पुरुषः कथं राष्ट्र मृतं भवेत् ।
श्राद्धं मृतं कथं वा स्यात् कथं यज्ञो मृतो भवेत् ॥ 3.313.83

yaksa uvaca
mritah katham syat purusah katham rastram mritam bhavet
sraddham mritam katham va syat katham yajno mrito bhavet
—3.313.83

Simple meaning—Yaksa asked, "Because of what may one be considered as dead, because of what may a kingdom be considered as dead, because of what may an ancestral worshipping ceremony be considered as dead, and because of what may a yajna be considered as dead?"

युधिष्ठिर उवाच

मृतो दरिद्रः पुरुषो मृतं राष्ट्रमराजकम् ।
मृतमश्रोत्रियं श्राद्धं मृतो यज्ञस्त्वदक्षिणः ॥ 3.313.84

yudhisthira uvaca

mrito daridrah puruso mritam rastramarajakam
mritamasrotriyam sraddham mrito yajnastvadaksinah

—3.313.84

Simple meaning—Yudhisthira replied, "Because of poverty may one be considered as dead, because of anarchy may a kingdom be considered as dead, because of lack of learning of the priest may an ancestral worshipping ceremony be considered as dead, and because of lack of respect may a yajna be considered as dead."

9.25 यक्ष उवाच

का दिक् किमुदकं प्रोक्तं किमन्नं किं च वै विषम् ।
श्राद्धस्य कालमाख्याहि ततः पिब हरस्व च ॥ 3.313.85

yaksa uvaca

ka dik kimudakam proktam kimannam kimca vai visam
sraddhasya kalamakhyahi tatah piba harasva ca

—3.313.85

Simple meaning—Yaksa asked, "Who shows the way, what has been spoken of as water by the Vedas, what has been spoken of as food, what is poison, and what is the proper time for performing an ancestral worshipping ceremony? Then you may drink water and also take away as much as you like."

युधिष्ठिर उवाच

सन्तो दिग् जलमाकाशं गौरन्नं प्रार्थना विषम् ।
श्राद्धस्य ब्राह्मणः कालः कथं वा यक्ष मन्यसे ॥ 3.313.86

yudhisthira uvaca
santo dig jalamakasam gaurannam prarthana visam
sraddhasya brahmanah kalah katham va yaksa manyase
—3.313.86

Simple meaning—Yudhisthira replied, "Good people show the way, space has been spoken of as water by the Vedas, earth has been spoken of as food, to ask for something is poison, and the proper time for performing an ancestral worshipping ceremony depends on the availability of a learned priest. I wonder what your opinion is."

9.26 यक्ष उवाच
तप: किंलक्षणं प्रोक्तं को दमश्च प्रकीर्तित: ।
क्षमा च का परा प्रोक्ता का च ह्री: परिकीर्तित: ॥ 3.313.87
yaksa uvaca
tapah kimlaksanam proktam ko damasca prakirtitah
ksama ca ka para prokta ka ca hrih parikirtitah
—3.313.87

Simple meaning—Yaksa asked, "What is tapas, what is the best type of restraint, what constitutes forgiveness, and what is the appropriate concept of shame?"

युधिष्ठिर उवाच
तप: स्वधर्मवर्तित्वं मनसो दमनं दम: ।
क्षमा द्वन्द्वसहिष्णुत्वं ह्रीरकार्यनिवर्तनम् ॥ 3.313.88
yudhisthira uvaca
tapah svadharmavartitvam manaso damanam damah
ksama dvandvasahisnutvam hrirakaryanivartanam
—3.313.88

Simple meaning—Yudhisthira replied, "Tapas is commitment to one's duty, restraint of the mind is the best type of restraint, forgiveness consists in enduring dualities, and the appropriate concept of shame is to stay away from all unworthy acts."

9.27 यक्ष उवाच

किं ज्ञानं प्रोच्यते राजन् कः शमश्च प्रकीर्तितः ।
दया च का परा प्रोक्ता किं चार्जवमुदाहृतम् ॥ 3.313.89

yaksa uvaca
kim jnanam procyate rajan kah samasca prakirtitah
daya ca ka para prokta kim carjavamudahritam
—3.313.89

Simple meaning—Yaksa asked, "What is knowledge, what is the best type of serenity, what constitutes compassion, and what is the appropriate concept of uprightness?"

युधिष्ठिर उवाच

ज्ञानं तत्त्वार्थसम्बोधः शमश्चित्तप्रशान्तता ।
दया सर्वसुखैषित्वमार्जवं समचित्तता ॥ 3.313.90

yudhisthira uvaca
jnanam tattvarthasambodhah samascittaprasantata
daya sarvasukhaisitvamarjavam samacittata
—3.313.90

Simple meaning—Yudhisthira replied, "Knowledge is the right understanding of the divine principle, tranquility of thoughts is the best type of serenity, compassion consists in wishing happiness of all, and even-mindedness is the appropriate concept of uprightness."

9.28 यक्ष उवाच

कः शत्रुर्दुर्जयः पुंसां कश्च व्याधिरनन्तकः ।
कीदृशश्च स्मृतः साधुरसाधुः कीदृशः स्मृतः ॥ 3.313.91

yaksa uvaca
kah satrurdurjayah pumsam kasca vyadhiranantakah
kidrisasca smritah sadhurasadhuh kidrisah smritah
—3.313.91

Simple meaning—Yaksa asked, "What enemy is difficult to conquer, what disease is endless, whom would you call a good person, and whom would you call a bad person?"

युधिष्ठिर उवाच

क्रोधः सुदुर्जयः शत्रुर्लोभो व्याधिरनन्तकः ।
सर्वभूतहितः साधुरसाधुर्निर्दय : स्मृतः ॥ 3.313.92

yudhisthira uvaca

krodhah sudurjayah satrurlobho vyadhiranantakah
sarvabhutahitah sadhurasadhurnirdayah smritah

—3.313.92

Simple meaning—Yudhisthira replied, "Anger is the enemy that is difficult to conquer, greed is an endless disease, a good person is one who does good to all, and lack of compassion is the main characteristic of a bad person."

9.29 यक्ष उवाच

को मोहः प्रोच्यते राजन् कश्च मानः प्रकीर्तितः ।
किमालस्यं च विज्ञेयं कश्च शोकः प्रकीर्तितः ॥ 3.313.93

yaksa uvaca

ko mohah procyate rajan kasca manah prakirtitah
kimalasyam ca vijneyam kasca sokah prakirtitah

—3.313.93

Simple meaning—Yaksa asked, "What is delusion, what is pride, what is laziness, and what is grief."

युधिष्ठिर उवाच

मोहो हि धर्ममूढत्वं मानस्त्वात्माभिमानिता ।
धर्मनिष्क्रियताऽलस्यं शोकस्त्वज्ञानमुच्यते ॥ 3.313.94

yudhisthira uvaca

moho hi dharmamudhatvam manastvatmabhimanita
dharmaniskriyatalasyam sokastvajnanamucyate

—3.313.94

Simple meaning—Yudhisthira replied, "Delusion means being confused about one's duty, pride consists in self-recognition, laziness means not discharging one's duty, and grief is the sure outcome of ignorance."

9.30 यक्ष उवाच

किं स्थैर्यमृषिभिः प्रोक्तं किं च धैर्यमुदाहृतम् ।
स्नानं च किं परं प्रोक्तं दानं च किमिहोच्यते ॥ 3.313.95

yaksa uvacca

kim sthairyamrisibhih proktam kim ca dhairyamudahritam
snanam ca kim param proktam danam ca kimihocyate
—3.313.95

Simple meaning—Yaksa asked, "What type of steadiness do the Rishi's admire, what form does one's patience take, what is the concept of cleaning, and what is the main object of giving or sharing?"

युधिष्ठिर उवाच

स्वधर्मे स्थिरता स्थैर्यं धैर्यमिन्द्रियनिग्रहः ।
स्नानं मनोमलत्यागो दानं वै भूतरक्षणम् ॥ 3.313.96

yudhisthira uvaca

svadharme sthirata sthairyam dhairyamindriyanigrahah
snanam manomalatyago danam vai bhutaraksanam
—3.313.96

Simple meaning—Yudhisthira replied, "Real steadiness is a non wavering commitment to one's duty, real patience is continued effort towards self - discipline, real cleanliness means getting rid of the impurities of the mind, and to protect all the creatures is the main object of giving or sharing."

9.31 यक्ष उवाच

कः पण्डितः पुमाञ्ज्ञेयो नास्तिकः कश्च उच्यते ।
को मूर्खः कश्च कामः स्यात् को मत्सर इति स्मृतः ॥ 3.313.97

yaksa uvaca

kah panditah pumanjneyo nastikah kasca ucyate
ko murkhah kasca kamah syat ko matsara iti smritah
—3.313.97

Simple meaning—Yaksa asked, "Who should be regarded as learned, who should be called an atheist, who should be called ignorant, what is the role of desire, and what is envy?"

युधिष्ठिर उवाच

धर्मज्ञः पण्डितो ज्ञेयो नास्तिको मूर्ख उच्यते ।
कामः संसारहेतुश्च हृत्तापो मत्सरः स्मृतः ॥ 3.313.98

yudhisthira uvaca

dharmajnah pandito jneyo nastiko murkha ucyate
kamah samsarahetusca hrittapo matsarah smritah
—3.313.98

Simple meaning—Yudhisthira replied, "One who knows his duty should be regarded as learned, one who is ignorant should be called an atheist, also one who is an atheist should be called ignorant, desire is the root cause of repeated cycle of births and deaths, and envy is the feeling of ill-will that burns your heart."

9.32 यक्ष उवाच

कोऽहंकार इति प्रोक्तः कश्च दम्भः प्रकीर्तितः ।
किं तद् दैवं परं प्रोक्तं किं तत् पैशुन्यमुच्यते ॥ 3.313.99

yaksa uvaca

kohankara iti proktah kasca dambhah prakirtitah
kim tad daivam param proktam kim tat paisunyamucyate
—3.313.99

Simple meaning—Yaksa asked, "What is egotism, what is hypocrisy, what is called the grace of gods, and what is malicious talk?"

युधिष्ठिर उवाच

महाज्ञानमहंकारो दम्भो धर्मो ध्वजोच्छ्रयः ।
दैवं दानफलं प्रोक्तं पैशुन्यं परदूषणम् ॥ 3.313.100

yudhisthira uvaca

mahajnanamhankaro dambho dharmo dhvajocchrayah
daivam danaphalam proktam paisunyam paradusanam
—3.313.100

Simple meaning—Yudhisthira replied, "Egotism is an expression of utter ignorance, hypocrisy consists in pretending as if you are the standard-bearer of dharma, what we call the grace of gods is in reality the fruit of what we have given to others, and malicious talk consists in speaking ill of others."

9.33 यक्ष उवाच

धर्मश्चार्थश्च कामश्च परस्परविरोधिनः ।
एषां नित्यविरुद्धानां कथमेकत्र संगमः ॥ 3.313.101

yaksa uvaca
dharmascarthasca kamasca parasparavirodhinah
esam nityaviruddhanam kathamekatra sangamah
—3.313.101

Simple meaning—Yaksa asked, "The three goals of life, viz. dharma, artha, and kama, are opposed to one another. How can these three exist together?"

यधिष्ठिर उवाच

यदा धर्मश्च भार्या च परस्परवशानुगौ ।
तदा धर्मार्थकामानां त्रयाणामपि संगमः ॥ 3.313.102

yudhisthira uvaca
yada dharmasca bharya ca parasparavasanugau
tada dharmarthakamanam trayanamapi sangamah
—3.313.102

Simple meaning—Yudhisthira replied, "When a man and his wife together become devoted to dharma, then the three goals of life can exist together."

9.34 यक्ष उवाच

अक्षयो नरकः केन प्राप्यते भरतर्षभ ।
एतन्मे पृच्छतः प्रश्नं तच्छीघ्रं वक्तुमर्हसि ॥ 3.313.103

yaksa uvaca
aksayo narakah kena prapyate bharatarsabha
etanme pricchatah prasnam tacchigram vaktumarhasi
—3.313.103

Simple meaning—Yaksa asked, "Who is he that is condemned to everlasting hell? Can you answer this question quickly?"

युधिष्ठिर उवाच

ब्राह्मणं स्वयमाहूय याचमानमकिंचनम् ।

पश्चान्नास्तीति यो ब्रूयात् सोऽक्षयं नरकं व्रजेत् ॥ 3.313.104

yudhisthira uvaca

brahmanam svayamahuya yacamanamakincanam

pascannastiti yo bruyat soksayam narakam brajet

—3.313.104

Simple meaning—Yudhisthira replied, "He who invites a poor brahmin, promising to make him a nice gift, but then tells him that he has nothing to give, goes to everlasting hell. (I want to mention two other types of persons who go to everlasting hell)."

वेदेषु धर्मशास्त्रेषु मिथ्या यो वै द्विजातिषु ।

देवेषु पितृधर्मेषु सोऽक्षयं नरकं व्रजेत् ॥ 3.313.105

vedesu dharmasastresu mithya yo vai dvijatisu

devesu pitridharmesu soksayam narakam vrajet

—3.313.105

Simple meaning—Yudhisthira continued, "He who imputes falsehood to, and shows disrespect towards, other scriptures, brahmins, God, and ceremonies in honour of the ancestors, goes to everlasting hell."

विद्यमाने धने लोभाद् दानभोगविवर्जितः ।

पश्चान्नास्तीति यो ब्रूयात् सोऽक्षयं नरकं व्रजेत् ॥ 3.313.106

vidyamane dhane lobhad danabhogavivarjitah

pascannastiti yo bruyat soksayam narakam vrajet

—3.313.106

Simple meaning—Yudhisthira concluded his reply about everlasting hell, "He also goes to everlasting hell who, inspite of having money, but because of greed, does three things, viz. *(i)* does not give in charity, *(ii)* does not spend money on pleasures that are consistent with dharma, and *(iii)* when approached by persons in need, tells them that he has nothing to give."

9.35 यक्ष उवाच

राजन् कुलेन वृत्तेन स्वाध्यायेन श्रुतेन वा।
ब्राह्मण्यं केन भवति प्रब्रूह्येतत् सुनिश्चितम्॥ 3.313.107

yaksa uvaca
rajan kulene vrittena svadhyayena srutena va
brahmanyam kena bhavati prabruhyetat suniscitam
—3.313.107

Simple meaning—Yaksa asked, "Out of the four factors, viz. family, conduct, self-study, and listening to scriptures—which one contributes to brahminhood? Can you give me a definite answer?"

युधिष्ठिर उवाच

शृणु यक्ष कुलं तात न स्वाध्यायो न च श्रुतम्।
कारणं हि द्विजत्वे च वृत्तमेव न संशयः॥ 3.313.108

yudhisthira uvaca
srinu yaksa kulam tata na svadhyayo na ca srutam
karanam hi dvijatve ca vrittameva na samsayah
—3.313.108

Simple meaning—Yudhisthira replied, "I can say without any doubt that, out of the four factors that you menioned, only one, viz. conduct, contributes to brahminhood-and the other three, viz. family, self-study, and listening to scriptures, are not so important. (And I want to explain this further)."

वृत्तं यत्नेन संरक्ष्यं ब्राह्मणेन विशेषतः।
अक्षीणवृत्तो न क्षीणो वृत्ततस्तु हतो हतः॥ 3.313.109

vrittam yatnena samraksyam brahmanena visesatah
aksinavritto na ksino vrittatastu hato hatah
—3.313.109

Simple meaning—Yudhisthira added, "One's good conduct should always be maintained, and full effort should be devoted to this goal, particularly by a brahmin. One who maintains good conduct loses nothing, but one who loses his conduct loses everything."

पठका: पाठकाश्चैव ये चान्ये शास्त्रचिन्तका: ।
सर्वे व्यसनिनो मूर्खा य: क्रियावान् स पण्डित: ॥ 3.313.110

pathakah pathakascaiva ye canye sastracintakah
sarve vyasanino murkha yah kriyavan sa panditah
—3.313.110

Simple meaning—Yudhisthira continued, "Even those who study the scriptures all the time, whether for self-study or for teaching, if their conduct is bad, they can be called ignorant and addicted. Only one whose conduct is good can be called learned."

चतुर्वेदोऽपि दुर्वृत्त: स शूद्रादतिरिच्यते ।
योऽग्निहोत्रपरो दान्त: स ब्राह्मण इति स्मृत: ॥ 3.313.111

caturvedopi durvrittah sa sudradatiricyate
yognihotraparo dantah sa brahmana iti smritah
—3.313.111

Simple meaning—Yudhisthira concluded his reply about brahminhood, "He whose conduct is bad, even if he knows all the four Vedas, is inferior to a sudra (*i.e.* a person of the lowest caste). On the other hand, he whose conduct is good (*i.e.* who performs his duty and who keeps his senses under control) is surely a brahmin."

9.36 यक्ष उवाच

प्रियवचनवादी किं लभते
विमृशितकार्यकर: किं लभते ।
बहुमित्रकर: किं लभते
धर्मरत: किं लभते कथय ॥ 3.313.112

yaksa uvaca
priyavacanavadi kim labhate
vimrisitakaryakarah kim labhate
bahumitrakarah kim labhate
dharmaratah kim labhate kathaya
—3.313.112

Simple meaning—Yaksa asked, "What does one gain who speaks sweet words, what does one gain who acts after considering the matter fully, what does one gain who makes many friends, and what does one gain who is devoted to righteousness?"

युधिष्ठिर उवाच

प्रियवचनवादी प्रियो भवति
विमृशितकार्यकरोऽधिकं जयति ।
बहुमित्रकरः सुखं वसते
यश्च धर्मरतः स गतिं लभते ॥ 3.313.113

yudhisthira uvaca
priyavacanavadi priyo bhavati
vimrisitakaryakarodhikam jayati
bahumitrakarah sukham vasate
yasca dharmaratah sa gatim labhate
—3.313.113

Simple meaning—Yudhisthira replied, "One who speaks sweet words endears oneself to all, one who acts after considering the matter fully has a very good chance of achieving success, one who makes many friends lives happily, and one who is devoted to righteousness attains a state of bliss."

9.37 यक्ष उवाच

को मोदते किमाश्चर्यं कः पन्थाः का च वार्तिका ।
ममैतांश्चतुरः प्रश्नान् कथयित्वा जलं पिब ॥ 3.313.114

yaksa uvaca
ko modate kimascaryam kah panthah ka ca vartika
mamaitamscaturah prasnan kathayitva jalam piba
—3.313.114

Simple meaning—Yaksa said, "Who lives joyfully, what is the greatest wonder, which is the right path to be followed, and what sort of conversation is full of meaning? After answering these four questions of mine, you may drink water."

युधिष्ठिर उवाच

पंचमेऽहनि षष्ठे वा शाकं पचति स्वे गृहे ।
अनृणी चाप्रवासी च स वारिचर मोदते ॥ 3.313.115

yudhisthira uvaca
pancamehani sasthe va sakam pacati sve grihe
anrini capravasi ca sa varicara modate

—3.313.115

Simple meaning—Yudhisthira replied, "One who is not burdened with debt, and who is not away from home, lives joyfully, even if he eats only vegetables, cooked at home every fifth or sixth day."

अहन्यहनि भूतानि गच्छन्तीह यमालयम् ।
शेषाः स्थावरमिच्छन्ति किमाश्चर्यमतः परम् ॥ 3.313.116
ahanyahani bhutani gacchantiha yamalayam
sesah sthavaramicchanti kimascaryamatah param

—3.313.116

Simple meaning—Yudhisthira continued, "People die every day, yet those who are alive, want to live for ever-this is the greatest wonder."

तर्कोऽप्रतिष्ठः श्रुतयो विभिन्ना
नैको ऋषिर्यस्य मतं प्रमाणम् ।
धर्मस्य तत्त्वं निहितं गुहायां
महाजनो येन गतः स पन्थाः ॥ 3.313.117
tarkopratisthah srutayo vibhinna
naiko risiryasya matam pramanam
dharmasya tattvam nihitam guhayam
mahajano yena gatah sa panthah

—3.313.117

Simple meaning—Yudhisthira went on, "About the right path to be followed, inferential logic alone cannot help in making a clear and good choice. In the Vedas and the Upanisads too, various answers to the same question can be found. As for the smrities, it is difficult to identify a single Rishi who can be considered more authoritative than others. So, in a way, it looks as if the essence of dharma is hidden in a cave. A practical solution to the problem is to follow the path shown by "Mahajana" (which has two meanings, viz. "a great person" or "a majority of people")."

अस्मिन् महामोहमये कटाहे
सूर्याग्निना रात्रिदिवेन्धनेन ।
मासर्तुदर्वीपरिघट्टनेन
भूतानि कालः पचतीति वार्ता ॥ 3.313.118

asmin mahamohamaye katahe
suryagnina ratridivendhanena
masartudarviparighattanena
bhutani kalah pacatiti varta

—3.313.118

Simple meaning—Yudhisthira concluded his reply to the four questions, "This world full of ignorance is like a pan. The sun is fire, the days and nights are fuel. The months and the seasons constitute the stirring spoon. Time is the cook. In this way, all the beings in this world are being cooked. This sort of conversation is full of meaning."

9.38 यक्ष उवाच

व्याख्याता मे त्वया प्रश्ना याथातथ्यं परंतप ।
पुरुषं त्विदानीं व्याख्याहि यश्च सर्वधनी नरः ॥ 3.313.119

yaksa uvaca
vyakhyata me tvaya prasna yathatathyam parantapa
purusam tvidanim vyakhyahi yasca sarvadhani narah

—3.313.119

Simple meaning—Yaksa said, "You have given right answers to all my questions. I now put two final questions – who is a purusa (*i.e.* a human being), and who can be said to possess limitless wealth?"

युधिष्ठिर उवाच

दिवं स्पृशति भूमिं च शब्दः पुण्येन कर्मणा ।
यावत् स शब्दो भवति तावत् पुरुष उच्यते ॥ 3.313.120

yudhisthira uvaca
divam sprisati bhumim ca sabdah punyena karmana
yavat sa sabdo bhavati tavat purusa ucyate

—3.313.120

Simple meaning—Yudhisthira replied to the first of the two questions, "The title "purusa" can be applied to a human being during that time when the popular appreciation of one's good actions spreads over the earth and reaches the heavens too."

तुल्ये प्रियाप्रिये यस्य सुखदुःखे तथैव च ।
अतीतानागते चोभे स वै सर्वधनी नरः ॥ 3.313.121

tulye priyapriye yasya sukhaduhkhe tathaiva ca
atitanagate cobhe sa vai sarvadhani narah

—3.313.121

Simple meaning—Yudhisthira replied to the second question (*i.e.* the last question of Yaksa), "One can be said to possess limitless wealth if one is even-minded under all situations, *i.e.* if the pleasant and the unpleasant, joys and sorrows, and even the past and future are the same to him or her."

9.39 यक्ष उवाच

व्याख्यातः पुरुषो राजन् यश्च सर्वधनी नरः ।
तस्मात् त्वमेकं भ्रातृणां यमिच्छसि स जीवतु ॥ 3.313.122

yaksa uvaca
vyakhyatah puruso rajan yasca sarvadhani narah
tasmat tvamekam bhratrinam yamicchasi sa jivatu

—3.313.122

Simple meaning—Yaksa said, "You have correctly answered both of my final questions. Therefore, I grant you a boon, viz. may one of your brothers, whom you choose, come back to life."

युधिष्ठिर उवाच

श्यामो य एष रक्ताक्षो बृहच्छाल इवोत्थितः ।
व्यूढोरस्को महाबाहुर्नकुलो यक्ष जीवतु ॥ 3.313.123

yudhisthira uvaca
syamo ya esa raktakso brihacchala ivotthitah
vyudhorasko mahabahurnakulo yaksa jivatu

—3.313.123

Simple meaning—Yudhisthira said, "Let this one who is of dark colour, whose eyes are red, who is tall like a tree, whose chest is broad and arms are long – let this Nakula come back to life."

9.40 यक्ष उवाच

प्रियस्ते भीमसेनोऽयमर्जुनो वः परायणम् ।
स कस्मान्नकुलं राजन् सापन्नं जीवमिच्छसि ॥ 3.313.124

yaksa uvaca
priyaste bhimasenoyamarjuno vah parayanam
sa kasmannakulam rajan sapannam jivamicchasi
—3.313.124

Simple meaning—Yaksa asked, "I am surprised at your choice. Why are you giving priority to Nakula (who is your step-brother) over Bhima and Arjuna – this Bhima who is dear to you, and this Arjuna on whom all of you depend?"

युधिष्ठिर उवाच
कुन्ती चैव तु माद्री च द्वे भार्ये तु पितुर्मम ।
उभे सपुत्रे स्यातां वै इति मे धीयते मतिः ॥ 3.313.131

yudhisthira uvaca
kunti caiva tu madri ca dve bharye tu piturmama
ubhe saputre syatam vai iti me dhiyate matih
—3.313.131

Simple meaning—Yudhisthira replied, "My father had two wives, Kunti and Madri. I want that at least one son of each of them should be alive."

यथा कुन्ती तथा माद्री विशेषो नास्ति मे तयोः ।
मातृभ्यां सममिच्छामि नकुलो यक्ष जीवतु ॥ 3.313.132

yatha kunti tatha madri viseso nasti me tayoh
matribhyam samamicchami nakulo yaksa jivatu
—3.313.132

Simple meaning—Yudhisthira concluded his reply about his choice of Nakula, "Although Kunti is my mother, I do not make any distinction between her and Madri – both are the same to me. Because of this view of mine, I have given priority to Madri's son Nakula, and I want him to come back to life."

9.41 यक्ष उवाच

तस्य तेऽर्थाच्च कामाच्च आनृशंस्यं परं मतम् ।
तस्मात् ते भ्रातर: सर्वे जीवन्तु भरतर्षभ ॥ 3.313.133

yaksa uvaca
tasya terthacca kamacca anrisamsyam param matam
tasmat te`bhratarah sarve jivantu bharatarsabha
—3.313.133

Simple meaning—Yaksa said to Yudhisthira, "You have demonstrated your highest devotion to 'absence of cruelty' - even higher than to artha and kama. Therefore, I grant you a boon, viz. may all your brothers come back to life."

This is how Yudhisthira brought his brothers back to life.

Chapter 10

How Shakuntala Protected Her Marriage and Her Son

10.1 The crisis which Shakuntala faced, although not presenting a straight forward life-and-death situation, was still very serious because its long-term impact on her own life as well as on her son's life, would have been devastating. She was married to King Dushyanta in Rishi Kanva's Ashrama, but subsequently when she and her son went to the kingdom's capital, the king pretended as if he did not even know her. The way Shakuntala argued her case, was so effective as to receive incontrovertible support from a heavenly voice. Then the king apologized for his unjust behaviour, and best owed full honours on Shakuntala, giving due recognition and love to the son too. Although Shakuntala's story is narrated in Parva No. 1 (Adi Parva), it fits neatly into the text of Apad-dharma. The Sanskrit dramatist Kalidasa presented the Mahabharata - version in the form of a play which attracted the world's scholars to the greatness of Shakuntala.

10.2 Shakuntala was the daughter of Rishi Vishvamitra, her mother being Menaka, a heavenly nymph. But Shakuntala was brought up by Rishi Kanva who found her, as an infant, on the banks of the river Malini. Kanva gave her the name 'Shakuntala' because she was protected by Shakunta - birds.

निर्जने तु वने यस्माच्छकुन्तैः परिवारिता ।
शकुन्तलेति नामास्याः कृतं चापि ततो मया ॥ 1.72.16

nirjane tu vane yasmacchakuntaih parivarita
sakuntaleti namasyah kritam capi tato maya
—1.72.16

Simple meaning—Rishi Kanva says, "In a forest, away from human habitation, I found this baby who was protected by Shakunta - birds, therefore I gave her the name "Shakuntala"."

10.3 Adi Parva describes how king Dushyanta, during the course of a hunting expedition, visited the Ashrama of Rishi Kanva.

दिदृक्षुस्तत्र तमृषिं तपोराशिमथाव्ययम् ।
क्षुत्पिपासे जहौ राजा मुदं चावाप पुष्कलाम् ॥ 1.70.36

didriksustatra tamrisim taporasimathavyayam
ksutpipase jahau raja mudam cavapa puskalam
—1.70.36

Simple meaning—The king wanted to meet Rishi Kanva and see his Ashrama which was well known as an educational center. As soon as the king saw the beautiful garden of the Ashrama, his hunger and thirst bothered him no more.

सोऽपश्यमानस्तमृषिं शून्यं दृष्ट्वा तथाऽश्रमम् ।
उवाच क इहेत्युच्चैर्वनं संनादयन्निव ॥ 1.71.2

sopasyamanastamrisim sunyam dristva tathasramam
uvaca ka ihetyuccairvanam samnadayanniva
—1.71.2

Simple meaning—In the absence of Rishi Kanva (who was not in the Ashrama at that time), it appeared to the king as if the Ashrama was empty. He then called loudly, "Is any one here?"

श्रुत्वाथ तस्य तं शब्दं कन्या श्रीरिव रूपिणी ।
निश्चक्रामाश्रमात् तस्मात् तापसीवेषधारिणी ॥ 1.71.3

srutvatha tasya tam sabdam kanya sririva rupini
niscakramasramat tasmat tapasivesadharini
—1.71.3

Simple meaning—Upon hearing a human voice, there came out of the Rishi's abode, a maiden of unsurpassed beauty who was dressed like the Rishi's daughter.

विस्पष्टं मधुरां वाचं साब्रवीज्जनमेजय ।
स्वागतं त इति क्षिप्रमुवाच प्रतिपूज्य च ॥ 1.71.4
उवाच स्मयमानेव किं कार्यं क्रियतामिति ।
कस्त्वमद्येह सम्प्राप्तो महर्षेराश्रमं शुभम् ॥ 1.71.6

vispastam madhuram vacam sabravijjanamejaya
svagatam ta iti ksipramuvaca pratipujya ca
—1.71.4
uvaca smayamaneva kim karyam kriyatamiti
kastvamadyeha samprapto maharserasramam subham
—1.71.6

Simple meaning—The maiden spoke to the king in sweet and clear voice, "Honourable visitor, I welcome you to the Ashrama. What can I do for you to help you fulfil the purpose of your visit?"

दुष्यन्त उवाच

राजर्षेरस्मि पुत्रोऽहमिलिलस्य महात्मनः ।
दुष्यन्त इति मे नाम सत्यं पुष्करलोचने ॥ 1.71.7
आगतोऽहं महाभागमृषिं कण्वमुपासितुम् ।
क्व गतो भगवान् भद्रे तन्ममाचक्ष्व शोभने ॥ 1.71.8

dusyanta uvaca
rajarserasmi putrohamililasya mahatmanah
dusyanta iti me nama satyam puskaralocane
—1.71.7
agatoham mahabhagamrisim kanvamupasitum
kva gato bhagavan bhadre tanmamacaksva sobhane
—1.71.8

Simple meaning—Dushyanta said, "I have come here to pay my respect to Rishi Kanva. My name is Dushyanta, and I am the son of Mahatma Ilila. It seems Rishi Kanva is not in the Ashrama now. May I know where he has gone and when he is likely to be back."

शकुन्तलोवाच
गतः पिता मे भगवान् फलान्याहर्तुमाश्रमात् ।
मुहूर्तं सम्प्रतीक्षस्व द्रष्टास्येनमुपागतम् ॥ 1.71.9

sakuntalovaca
gatah pita me bhagavan phalanyahartumasramat
muhurtam sampratiksasva drastasyenamupagatam
—1.71.9

Simple meaning—Shakuntala said, "My illustrious father has gone out to get some fruits. Please wait, he should be here soon."

10.4 While Dushyanta and Shakuntala were waiting for Rishi Kanva to arrive, they exchanged information about each other.

दुष्यन्त उवाच
दर्शनादेव हि शुभे त्वया मेऽपहृतं मनः ।
इच्छामि त्वामहं ज्ञातुं तन्ममाचक्ष्व शोभने ॥ 1.71.13

dusyanta uvaca
darsanadeva hi subhe tvaya mepahritam manah
icchami tvamaham jnatum tanmamacaksva sobhane
—1.71.13

Simple meaning—Dushyanta said, "My heart feels immense attraction for you. Please tell me more about yourself."

10.5 Having heard details about Shakuntala's birth and early life, the King proposed to her that they should get married according to 'Gandharva form' (i.e. mutual consent).

दुष्यन्त उवाच
सुव्यक्तं राजपुत्री त्वं यथा कल्याणि भाषसे ।
भार्या मे भव सुश्रोणि ब्रूहि किं करवाणि ते ॥ 1.73.1
गान्धर्वेण च मां भीरु विवाहेनैहि सुन्दरि ।
विवाहानां हि रम्भोरु गान्धर्वः श्रेष्ठ उच्यते ॥ 1.73.4

dusyanta uvaca
suvyaktam rajaputri tvam yatha kalyani bhasase
bharya me bhava susroni bruhi kim karavani te
—1.73.1

gandharvena ca mam bhiru vivahenaihi sundari
vivahanam hi rambhoru gandharvah srestha ucyate
—1.73.4

Simple meaning—Dushyanta said to Shakuntala, "Sweet lady, as you told me, you are the daughter of Vishvamitra, and hence a ksatriya. Please accept my proposal and be my wife. I will do everything to ensure your happiness. I propose that we get married according to 'Gandharva form' i.e. mutual consent."

10.6 But Shakuntala placed a condition.

शकुन्तलोवाच
यदि धर्मपथस्त्वेष यदि चात्मा प्रभुर्मम ।
प्रदाने पौरवश्रेष्ठ शृणु मे समयं प्रभो ॥ 1.73.15
सत्यं मे प्रतिजानीहि यथा वक्ष्याम्यहं रहः ।
मयि जायेत यः पुत्रः स भवेत् त्वदनन्तरः ॥ 1.73.16
युवराजो महाराज सत्यमेतद् ब्रवीमि ते ।
यद्येतदेवं दुष्यन्त अस्तु मे संगमस्त्वया ॥ 1.73.17

sakuntalovaca
yadi dharmapathastvesa yadi catma prabhurmama
pradane pauravasrestha srinu me samayam prabho
—1.73.15

satyam me pratijanihi yatha vaksyamyaham rahah
mayi jayeta yah putrah sa bhavet tvadanantarah
—1.73.16

yuvarajo maharaja satyametad bravimi te
yadyetadevam dusyanta astu me sangamastvaya
—1.73.17

Simple meaning—Shakuntala said, "O King Dushyanta, if the Gandharva form of marriage, as proposed by you, is in accordance with dharma, then I give my consent, but I want to put one condition. Although there is no other witness here, you have to give me your word that you accept my condition, viz. that if I give birth to a son, then he will succeed you on the throne. I am speaking from my heart, and if you too declare your firm acceptance of my condition, then we can get married."

10.7 दुष्यन्त उवाच

एवमस्त्विति तां राजा प्रत्युवाचाविचारयन् ।
अपि च त्वां हि नेष्यामि नगरं स्वं शुचिस्मिते ॥ 1.73.18

dusyanta uvaca
evamastviti tam raja pratyuvacavicarayan
api ca tvam hi nesyami nagaram svam sucismite
—1.73.18

Simple meaning—King Dushyanta joyfully replied to Shakuntala, "Righteous lady, I accept your condition whole -heartedly. In fact, I will come here and both of us will then move to the capital city of my kingdom."

10.8 Having got married to Shakuntala, the king stayed with her at the Ashrama for some time, and then returned to his kingdom. Rishi Kanva gave his blessings to Shakuntala and continued to look after her as also the son to whom she gave birth.

कण्व उवाच

धर्मात्मा च महात्मा च दुष्यन्तः परुषोत्तमः ॥ 1.73.28
महात्मा जनिता लोके पुत्रस्तव महाबलः ।
स इमां सागरापांगीं कृत्स्नां भोक्ष्यति मेदिनीम् ॥ 1.73.29

kanva uvaca
dharmatma ca mahatma ca dusyantah purusottamah
1.73.28

mahatma janita loke putrastava mahabalah
sa imam sagarapangim kritsnam bhoksyati medinim
—1.73.29

Simple meaning—Rishi Kanva said to Shakuntala, "My dearest daughter, I am so happy that, after marrying Mahatma Dushyanta, you have given birth to a son who will prove to be a great and righteous king. My blessings to you as well as the son."

10.9 The birth of Shakuntala's son was a moment of great joy to Indra also.

शक्र उवाच

शकुन्तले तव सुतश्चक्रवर्ती भविष्यति ।
बलं तेजश्च रूपं च न समं भुवि केनचित् ॥ 1.74.3

sakra uvaca
sakuntale tava sutascakravarti bhavisyati
balam tejasca rupam ca na samam bhavi kenacit
—1.74.3

Simple meaning—Indra congratulated Shakuntala, "O great lady, your son will grow up to be a unique man, exercising sovereignty over a vast kingdom and taking excellent care of all the citizens."

10.10 Shakuntala's son grew up in the sanctified atmosphere of Kanva Rishi's Ashrama, under the care of all the members of the Ashrama - community.

ततोऽस्य नाम चक्रुस्ते कण्वाश्रमनिवासिनः ।
अस्त्वयं सर्वदमनः सर्वं हि दमयत्यसौ ।
स सर्वदमनो नाम कुमारः समपद्यत ॥ 1.74.8

tatosya nama cakruste kanvasramanivasinah
astvayam sarvadamanah sarvam hi damayatyasau
sa sarvadamano nama kumarah samapadyata
—1.74.8

Simple meaning—Residents of the Ashrama said, "We see all the time that this little boy can control all animals, therefore we feel that 'Sarvadamana' will be an appropriate name for him." So Shakuntala's son became known by this name.

10.11 Shakuntala waited for King Dushyanta to come to the Ashrama, as he had promised, but he did not show up. Then Rishi Kanva advised her to go to the kingdom's capital.

कण्व उवाच

तस्माद् भद्रे प्रयातव्यं समीपं पौरवस्य ह ।

स्वयं नायाति मत्वा ते गतं कालं शुचिस्मिते ।
गत्वाऽराधय राजानं दुष्यन्तं हितकाम्यया ॥ 1.74.10

kanva uvaca
tasmad bhadre prayatavyam samipam pauravasya ha
svayam nayati matva te gatam kalam sucismite
gatvaradhaya rajanam dusyantam hitakamyaya
—1.74.10

Simple meaning—Kanva Rishi said to Shakuntala, "My dearest daughter, you have waited for a long time, but now it is better that you yourself undertake the journey, along with Sarvadamana, to the Kingdom's capital."

10.12 In the capital city, when Shakuntala (with her son) saw King Dushyanta, she asked him to recall his visit to the Ashrama of Rishi Kanva.

शकुन्तलोवाच
अयं पुत्रस्त्वया राजन् यौवराज्येऽभिषिच्यताम् ।
त्वया ह्ययं सुतो राजन् मय्युत्पन्नः सुरोपमः ।
यथासमयमेतस्मिन् वर्तस्व पुरुषोत्तम ॥ 1.74.17

sakuntalovaca
ayam putrastvaya rajan yauvarajyebhisicyatam
tvaya hyayam suto rajan mayyutpannah suropamah
yathasamayametasmin vartasva purusottama
—1.74.17

Simple meaning—Shakuntala said to Dushyanta, "O king, here is your son. I gave birth to him in Kanva Rishi's Ashrama. According to the promise that you made at the time of our marriage, this boy will succeed you on the throne. But a declaration to that effect should be made now."

10.13 But Dushyanta's reply came as a big shock for Shakuntala.

सोऽथ श्रुत्वैव तद् वाक्यं तस्या राजा स्मरन्नपि ।
धर्मकामार्थसम्बन्धं न स्मरामि त्वया सह ॥ 1.74.19

sotha srutvaiva tad vakyam tasya raja smarannapi
dharmakamarthasambandham na smarami tvaya saha
—1.74.19

Simple meaning—Although the King fully remembered his visit to the Ashrama, still he pretended as if he did not even know Shakuntala.

10.14 आकारं गूहमाना च मन्युना च समीरिता ।
तपसा सम्भृतं तेजो धारयामास वै तदा ॥ 1.74.23
सा मुहूर्तमिव ध्यात्वा दुःखामर्षसमन्विता ।
भर्तारमभिसम्प्रेक्ष्य क्रुद्धा वचनमब्रवीत् ॥ 1.74.24
akaram guhamana ca manyuna ca samirita
tapasa sambhritam tejo dharayamasa vai tada
—1.74.23

sa muhurtamiva dhyatva duhkhamarsasamanvita
bhartaramabhisampreksya kruddha vacanamabravit
—1.74.24

Simple meaning—For a few seconds, anger took control of Shakuntala's heart, but then she was able to be calm and composed. Such was the strength of her character. She decided to speak firmly, to put pressure on the king to recall his visit to the Ashrama.

10.15 This was the moment which tested Shakuntala's capability to face the crisis. B. A. Van Nooten says, "Shakuntala, looking the king straight in the face, burst forth in an impassioned speech, one of the finest in the epic[1]."

शकुन्तलोवाच

जानन्नपि महाराज कस्मादेवं प्रभाषसे ।
न जानामीति निःशंकं यथान्यः प्राकृतो जनः ॥ 1.74.25
sakuntalovaca
janannapi maharaja kasmadevam prabhasase
na janamiti nihsankam yathanyah prakrito janah
—1.74.25

Simple meaning—Shakuntala said to Dushyanta, "O King, although you know the truth very well, why do you talk in this manner, saying like any commoner 'I do not know'."

अत्र ते हृदयं वेद सत्यस्यैवानृतस्य च ।
कल्याणं वद साक्ष्येण माऽत्मानमवमन्यथाः ॥ 1.74.26

atra te hridayam veda satyasyaivanritasya ca
kalyanam vada saksyena matmanamavamanyathah
—1.74.26

Simple meaning—"In this matter, I know, it is your heart that is witness to its truth or falsehood. Speak from your heart and that will be to your good - please do not degrade yourself."

एकोऽहमस्मीति च मन्यसे त्वं
न हृच्छयं वेत्सि मुनिं पुराणम् ।
यो वेदिता कर्मण: पापकस्य
तस्यान्तिके त्वं वृजिनं करोषि ॥ 1.74.28

ekohamasmiti ca manyase tvam
na hricchayam vetsi munim puranam
yo vedita karmanah papakasya
tasyantike tvam vrijinam karosi
—1.74.28

Simple meaning—"Please don't be misguided by the wrong notion that, besides you and me, there was no third person in the Ashrama at that time, because the omnipresent Brahman sees everything and knows everything. Your inner voice will ask you not to do anything wrong."

आदित्यचन्द्रावनिलानलौ च
द्यौर्भूमिरापो हृदयं यमश्च ।
अहश्च रात्रिश्च उभे च संध्ये
धर्मश्च जानाति नरस्य वृत्तम् ॥ 1.74.30

adityacandravanilanalau ca
dyaurbhumirapo hridayam yamasca
ahasca ratrisca ubhe ca sandhye
dharmasca janati narasya vrittam
—1.74.30

Simple meaning—"Vedas tell us that the sun, the moon, the earth, the sky, the day, the night, Yama and Dharma – through all these, the good as well as the bad deeds of human beings are constantly being watched by Brahman."

स्वयं प्राप्तेति मामेवं मावमंस्थाः पतिव्रताम् ।
अर्चार्हां नार्चयसि मां स्वयं भार्यामुपस्थिताम् ॥ 1.74.34

svayam prapteti mamevam mavamamsthah pativratam
arcarham narcayasi mam svayam bharyamupasthitam
—1.74.34

Simple meaning—"Please do not underestimate the high status of the wife in your life. I, as your wife, deserve to be honoured by you. Since you did not make your second visit to the Ashrama, as you had promised, I myself have come to you."

अर्धं भार्या मनुष्यस्य भार्या श्रेष्ठतमः सखा ।
भार्या मूलं त्रिवर्गस्य भार्यामूलं तरिष्यतः ॥ 1.74.41

ardham bharya manusyasya bharya sresthatamah sakha
bharya mulam trivargasya bharya mulam tarisyatah
—1.74.41

Simple meaning—"A man without wife is incomplete, because the contribution of the wife is equal to that of the man. Also the wife is the best friend. Our scriptures say that it is because of the wife that the family achieves the goals of life (artha, kama, dharma, and moksa).

कान्तारेष्वपि विश्रामो जनस्याध्वनिकस्य वै ।
यः सदारः स विश्वास्यस्तस्माद् दाराः परा गतिः ॥ 1.74.44

kantaresvapi visramo janasyadhvanikasya vai
yah sadarah sa visvasyastasmad darah para gatih
—1.74.44

Simple meaning—"Even in wilderness, a traveller accompanied with wife has greater security. In the society, a man who has a wife is trusted by everyone. Therefore, a wife helps in securing all the goals of life, whatever may be the circumstances."

राजन् सत्यं परं ब्रह्म सत्यं च समयः परः ।
मा त्याक्षीः समयं राजन् सत्यं संगतमस्तु ते ॥ 1.74.106

rajan satyam param brahma satyam ca samayah parah
ma tyaksih samayam rajan satyam sangatamastu te
—1.74.106

Simple meaning—"O King, all the statements that I have made are true, because Vedas say that Truth is God. You too should hold on to Truth, which means that you should fulfil the promise that you made to me in the Ashrama."

कामं त्वया परित्यक्ता गमिष्यामि स्वमाश्रमम् ।
इमं तु बालं संत्यक्तुं नार्हस्यात्मजमात्मनः ॥ 1.74.72

kamam tvaya parityakta gamisyami svamasramam
imam tu balam santyaktum narhasyatmajamatmanah
—1.74.72

Simple meaning—"O King, if you do not honour me, I shall go back to the Ashrama. But you will repent if you let go this little boy who is your own son."

त्वामृतेऽपि हि दुष्यन्त शैलराजावतंसकाम् ।
चतुरन्तामिमामुर्वीं पुत्रो मे पालयिष्यति ॥ 1.74.108

tvamritepi hi dusyanta sailarajavatamsakam
caturantamimamurvim putro me palayisyati
—1.74.108

Simple meaning—"O King, when this son of mine was born, the Rishis of the Ashrama blessed him and predicted that he will grow up to be a great king, exercising sovereignty over this vast land. You have the golden opportunity to accept him as your son and be a part of the greatness which God will bestow on him."

10.16 Shakuntala's statements received incontrovertible support from a heavenly voice which convinced the king as well as all others who were present there at that critical juncture.

अथान्तरिक्षाद् दुष्यन्तं वागुवाचाशरीरिणी ॥ 1.74.109
सुतोऽयं तव पौरव सत्यमाह शकुन्तला ।
भरस्व पुत्रं दुष्यन्त मावमंस्थाः शकुन्तलाम् ॥ 1.74.112
भर्तव्योऽयं त्वया यस्मादस्माकं वचनादपि ।
तस्माद् भवत्वयं नाम्ना भरतो नाम ते सुतः ॥ 1.74.115

athantariksad dusyantam vaguvacasaririni
—1.74.109

sutoyam tava paurava satyamaha sakuntala
bharasva putram dusyanta mavamamsthah sakuntalam
—1.74.112

bhartavyoyam tvaya yasmadasmakam vacanadapi
tasmad bhavatvayam namna bharato nama te sutah
—1.74.115

Simple meaning—The heavenly voice spoke to Dushyanta, "Shakuntala's statements are true, therefore do not show disrespect to her. This little boy is your own son, therefore accept him as such. Following our advice, you will provide 'bharanam' (i.e. support and protection) to this son of yours, so he will be known as 'Bharata'."

10.17 After hearing the heavenly voice, the king joyfully honoured Shakuntala as his wife, and accepted the little boy as his son.

तां चैव भार्यां दुष्यन्तः पूजयामास धर्मतः ॥ 1.74.121
हृष्टः प्रमुदितश्चापि प्रतिजग्राह तं सुतम् ॥ 1.74.118

tam caiva bharyam dusyantah pujayamasa dharmatah
—1.74.121

hristah pramuditascapi pratijagraha tam sutam
—1.74.118

Simple meaning—The king joyfully announced his acceptance of Shakuntala as his wife, and bestowed full honours on her. The King also announced his acceptance of the little boy as his son, and joyfully held him in his lap.

10.18 The King requested Shakuntala to forgive him for the improper way he had treated her, upon her arrival from the Ashrama.

दुष्यन्त उवाच

त्वयाप्येवं विशालाक्षि क्षन्तव्यं मम दुर्वचः ॥ 1.74.125

कृतो लोकपरोक्षोऽयं सम्बन्धो वै त्वया सह ।

तस्मादेतन्मया देवि त्वच्छुद्ध्यर्थं विचारितम् ॥ 1.74.122

dusyanta uvaca

tvayapyevam visalakshi ksantavyam mama durvacah
—1.74.125

krito lokaparoksoyam sambandho vai tvaya saha
tasmadetanmaya devi tvacchuddhyartham vicaritam
—1.74.122

Simple meaning—King Dushyanta spoke to Shakuntala, "O Devi (respectable lady like a goddess), please pardon me for all the harsh words that I spoke. It was all like a drama. This plan was devised by me so that the purity of our relationship may become known to all - otherwise they might have remained in the dark because no one else was present when we got married."

10.19 The King's mother, Rathantarya, welcomed Shakuntala to the royal household, and showered her blessings on the new queen.

पादयोः पतितां तत्र रथन्तर्या शकुन्तलाम् ।

उवाच वचनं सत्यं लक्षयँल्लक्षणानि च ॥ 1.74.126

padayoh patitam tatra rathantarya sakuntalam
uvaca vacanam satyam laksayamllaksanani ca
—1.74.126

Simple meaning—Shakuntala touched the feet of her mother-in-law, Rathantarya, who joyfully welcomed the daughter-in-law, as also the bright, little boy.

रथन्तर्योवाच

दिव्यान् भोगाननुप्राप्ता भव त्वं वरवर्णिनि ।

तव पुत्रो विशालाक्षि चक्रवर्ती भविष्यति ॥ 1.74.127

rathantaryovaca

divyan bhogananuprapta bhava tvam varavarnini
tava putro visalaksi cakravarti bhavisyati
—1.74.127

Simple meaning—The King's mother, Rathantarya, blessed Shakuntala, "O Laksmi (goddess) of our household, may God shower upon you all the joys of life. Your son, the new prince, will grow up to be a great king."

10.20 The qualities which Bharata (previously known as Sarvadamana) had acquired at Rishi Kanva's Ashrama, were further developed under the parental care of Shakuntala and Dushyanta. In due course of time, Bharata succeeded Dushyanta as a king but surpassed him – and all other ancient rulers too – so much so that the Sanskrit name of India, viz. 'Bharatavarsha' is derived from him. Shakuntala has been duly recognized as the mother who contributed so much to the building up of Bharata's character. If she had not faced the crisis situation in the spirit of Apad-dharma, all these happy developments would not have taken place[2].

Chapter 11

How Yudhisthira Achieved a Glorious End for Everyone

11.1 In chapter Nine, we described how Yudhisthira brought his brothers back to life. That occurrence relates to Yudhisthira's youth, and is narrated in Vana Parva (i.e. Parva No. 3). On the other hand, the events summarized in the present chapter occur towards the end of the Mahabharata, and are narrated in Mahaprasthanika Parva (i.e. Parva No. 17). The title of this Parva means 'The Great Departure', i.e. the final journey on foot, to high mountains and heaven, by the five Pandava brothers and their wife Draupadi (i.e. six in all). The Lord of Dharma assumed the form of a dog who became the seventh member of the walking team (although Yudhisthira was unaware of this drama). Draupadi and the four Pandavas could not complete the journey on foot, and fell down, one by one. Only Yudhisthira and the dog reached the gate of heaven. The problem facing Yudhisthira at that time was how to ensure a glorious end for every member of the walking team. For this, he had to enter into a dialogue with Indra, which is one of the finest sections of the Mahabharata. In the end, Yudhisthira achieved complete success.

11.2 युधिष्ठिरो ययावग्रे भीमस्तु तदनन्तरम् ।
अर्जुनस्तस्य चान्वेव यमौ चापि यथाक्रमम् ॥ **17.1.31**

yudhisthiro yayavagre bhimastu tadanantaram
arjunastasya canveva yamau capi yathakramam
—17.1.31

Simple meaning—Yudhisthira proceeded first. Behind him was Bhima, next walked Arjuna, and after him were the twins (Nakula and Sahadeva).

पृष्ठतस्तु वरारोहा श्यामा पद्मदलेक्षणा ।
द्रौपदी योषितां श्रेष्ठा ययौ भरतसत्तम ॥ 17.1.32

pristhatastu vararoha syama padmadaleksana
draupadi yositam srestha yayau bharatasattama
—17.1.32

Simple meaning—Behind these five, proceeded Draupadi, a great woman possessed of genuine beauty, of dark complexion, and endued with eyes resembling lotus petals.

श्वा चैवानुययावेकः प्रस्थितान् पाण्डवान् वनम् ।
क्रमेण ते ययुर्वीरा लौहित्यं सलिलार्णवम् ॥ 17.1.33

sva caivanuyayavekah prasthitan pandavan vanam
kramena te yayurvira lauhityam salilarnavam
—17.1.33

Simple meaning—While the Pandavas set out for the forest (en route to heaven), a dog followed them. Proceeding on, these heroes reached the sea of red waters.

ततस्ते तूत्तरेणैव तीरेण लवणाम्भसः ।
जग्मुर्भरतशार्दूल दिशं दक्षिणपश्चिमाम् ॥ 17.1.44

tataste tuttarenaiva tirena lavanambhasah
jagmurbharatasardula disam daksinapascimam
—17.1.44

Simple meaning—Walking on and on, they passed by the northern coast of the salt sea, and then proceeded to the south-west.

ततः पुनः समावृत्ताः पश्चिमां दिशमेव ते ।
ददृशुर्द्वारकां चापि सागरेण परिप्लुताम् ॥ 17.1.45

tatah punah samavrittah pascimam disameva te
dadrisurdvarakam capi sagarena pariplutam
—17.1.45

Simple meaning—Thereafter they turned towards the west. They beheld (from a distance) the city of Dwaraka which was at that time covered by the ocean.

उदीचीं पुनरावृत्य ययुर्भरतसत्तमाः ।
प्रादक्षिण्यं चिकीर्षन्तः पृथिव्या योगधर्मिणः ॥ 17.1.46
udicim punaravritya yayurbharatasattamah
pradaksinyam cikirsantah prithivya yogadharminah
—17.1.46

Simple meaning—Next, they turned to the north and walked on. All the time, they practiced yoga, and they thought of making a round of the whole earth (before proceeding to the final destination, i.e. heaven).

11.3 ततस्ते नियतात्मान उदीचीं दिशमास्थिताः ।
ददृशुर्योगयुक्ताश्च हिमवन्तं महागिरिम् ॥ 17.2.1
tataste niyatatmana udicim disamasthitah
dadrisuryogayuktasca himavantam mahagirim
—17.2.1

Simple meaning—Observing self-discipline and practicing yoga, the Pandavas walked north-ward till they saw the Himalaya mountains.

तं चाप्यतिक्रमन्तस्ते ददृशुर्वालुकार्णवम् ।
अवैक्षन्त महाशैलं मेरुं शिखरिणां वरम् ॥ 17.2.2
tam capyatikramantaste dadrisurvalukarnavam
avaiksanta mahasailam merum sikharinam varam
—17.2.2

Simple meaning—After crossing the Himalaya mountains, they beheld a vast desert of sand. Then they saw the mighty mountain Meru.

11.4 तेषां तु गच्छतां शीघ्रं सर्वेषां योगधर्मिणाम् ।
याज्ञसेनी भ्रष्टयोगा निपपात महीतले ॥ 17.2.3

tesam tu gacchatam sighram sarvesam yogadharminam
yajnaseni bhrastayoga nipapata mahitale

—17.2.3

Simple meaning—Because of concentration in yoga, all of them were proceeding quickly. However, suddenly Draupadi lost her concentration and dropped down on earth.

तां तु प्रपतितां दृष्ट्वा भीमसेनो महाबलः ।
उवाच धर्मराजानं याज्ञसेनीमवेक्ष्य ह ॥ 17.2.4

tam tu prapatitam dristva bhimaseno mahabalah
uvaca dharmarajanam yajnasenimaveksya ha

—17.2.4

Simple meaning—Beholding Draupadi fallen down, Bhima of great strength put a question to Yudhisthira (in whose practice of dharma, Bhima had great faith).

नाधर्मश्चरितः कश्चिद् राजपुत्र्या परंतप ।
कारणं किं नु तद् ब्रूहि यत् कृष्णा पतिता भुवि ॥ 17.2.5

nadharmascaritah kascid rajaputrya parantapa
karanam kim nu tad bruhi yat krisna patita bhuvi

—17.2.5

Simple meaning—Bhima asked Yudhisthira, "O learned brother, as far as I know, this princess (Draupadi) never did any sinful act. Can you please tell me the reason why such a pious soul has fallen down on earth."

युधिष्ठिर उवाच
पक्षपातो महानस्या विशेषेण धनंजये ।
तस्यैतत् फलमद्यैषा भुंक्ते पुरुषसत्तम ॥ 17.2.6

yudhisthira uvaca
paksapato mahanasya visesena dhananjaye
tasyaitat phalamadyaisa bhunkte purusasattama

—17.2.6

Simple meaning—Yudhisthira replied to Bhima, "My dear brother, a delicate psychological point is involved here. You know that we five brothers were Draupadi's husbands.

Although she loved each one of us, yet she had a lot of partiality for Arjuna. She has fallen today because of that fault of hers."

11.5 एवमुक्त्वानवेक्ष्यैनां ययौ भरतसत्तमः ।
समाधाय मनो धीमान् धर्मात्मा पुरुषर्षभः ॥ 17.2.7
evamuktvanaveksyainam yayau bharatasattamah
samadhaya mano dhiman dharmatma purusarsabhah
—17.2.7

Simple meaning—Having answered Bhima's question, and having reconciled himself to Draupadi's fall, the righteous souled Yudhisthira walked on. He maintained his concentration in yoga, and (as a sign of non - attachment), he did not look back towards Draupadi.

11.6 सहदेवस्ततो विद्वान् निपपात महीतले ।
तं चापि पतितं दृष्ट्वा भीमो राजानमब्रवीत् ॥ 17.2.8
sahadevastato vidvan nipapata mahitale
tam capi patitam dristva bhimo rajanamabravit
—17.2.8

Simple meaning—After some time, Sahadeva, the youngest brother who was very learned, fell down on earth. Beholding him fallen down, Bhima put a question to Yudhisthira (as he had done after Draupadi's fall).

योऽयमस्मासु सर्वेषु शुश्रुषुरनहंकृतः ।
सोऽयं माद्रवतीपुत्रः कस्मान् निपतितो भुवि ॥ 17.2.9
yoyamasmasu sarvesu susrusuranahamkritah
soyam madravatiputrah kasman nipatito bhuvi
—17.2.9

Simple meaning—Bhima asked Yudhisthira, "O learned brother, as far as I know, this youngest brother of ours (i.e. Sahadeva) served all of us with great humility. Can you please tell me the reason why such a fine soul has fallen down on earth."

युधिष्ठिर उवाच

आत्मनः सदृशं प्राज्ञं नैषोऽमन्यत कंचन ।
तेन दोषेण पतितस्तस्मादेष नृपात्मजः ॥ 17.2.10

yudhisthira uvaca
atmanah sadrisam prajnam naisomanyata kancana
tena dosena patitastasmadesa nripatmajah
—17.2.10

Simple meaning—Yudhisthira replied to Bhima, "My dear brother, I agree that our youngest brother Sahadeva served us well but he never thought of anybody as his equal in wisdom. It is because of that fault of his that today he has fallen down."

11.7 इत्युक्त्वा तं समुत्सृज्य सहदेवं ययौ तदा ।
भ्रातृभिः सह कौन्तेयः शुना चैव युधिष्ठिरः ॥ 17.2.11

ityuktva tam samutsrijya sahadevam yayau tada
bhratribhih saha kaunteyah suna caiva yudhisthirah
—17.2.11

Simple meaning—Having answered Bhima's question, and having reconciled himself to Sahadeva's fall, the righteous - souled Yudhisthira walked on, followed by three (surviving) brothers and the dog.

11.8 कृष्णां निपतितां दृष्ट्वा सहदेवं च पाण्डवम् ।
आर्तो बन्धुप्रियः शूरो नकुलो निपपात ह ॥ 17.2.12

krisnam nipatitam dristva sahadevam ca pandavam
arto bandhupriyah suro nakulo nipapata ha
—17.2.12

Simple meaning—Nakula, the youngest of the three surviving brothers, suddenly lost his concentration and fell down, because (although he was very brave) he was struck with grief at the loss of Draupadi and Sahadeva whom he loved dearly.

तस्मिन् निपतिते वीरे नकुले चारुदर्शने ।
पुनरेव तदा भीमो राजानमिदमब्रवीत् ॥ 17.2.13

tasmin nipatite vire nakule carudarsane
punareva tada bhimo rajanamidamabravit

—17.2.13

Simple meaning—Upon the falling down of the heroic Nakula of great personal beauty, Bhima once more put a question to Yudhisthira (as he had done after the fall of Draupadi and Sahadeva).

योऽयमक्षतधर्मात्मा भ्राता वचनकारकः ।
रूपेणाप्रतिमो लोके नकुलः पतितो भुवि ॥ 17.2.14

yoyamaksatadharmatma bhrata vacanakarakah
rupenapratimo loke nakulah patito bhuvi

—17.2.14

Simple meaning—Bhima asked Yudhisthira, "O learned brother as far as I know, this brother of ours (i.e. Nakula), in spite of having unrivalled beauty, practiced dharma faultlessly and always carried out our wishes. Can you please tell me the reason why such a fine soul has fallen down on earth."

इत्युक्तो भीमसेनेन प्रत्युवाच युधिष्ठिरः ।
नकुलं प्रति धर्मात्मा सर्वबुद्धिमतां वरः ॥ 17.2.15

ityukto bhimasenena pratyuvaca yudhisthirah
nakulam prati dharmatma sarvabuddhimatam varah

—17.2.15

Simple meaning—After listening to Bhima's question, the righteous - souled Yudhisthira, endowed with the highest wisdom, pondered over the cause of Nakula's fall and conveyed it to Bhima in the following words.

युधिष्ठिर उवाच

रूपेण मत्समो नास्ति कश्चिदित्यस्य दर्शनम् ।
अधिकश्चाहमेवैक इत्यस्य मनसि स्थितम् ॥ 17.2.16
नकुलः पतितस्तस्मादागच्छ त्वं वृकोदर ।
यस्य यद् विहितं वीर सोऽवश्यं तदुपाश्नुते ॥ 17.2.17

yudhisthira uvaca
rupena matsamo nasti kascidityasya darsanam
adhikascahamevaika ityasya manasi sthitam

—17.2.16

nakulah patitastasmadagaccha tvam vrikodara
yasya yad vihitam vira sovasyam tadupasnute

—17.2.17

Simple meaning—Yudhisthira replied to Bhima, "My dear brother, I agree with what you said about Nakula, but I have to point out one fault of his, viz. that he thought there was no one that equalled him in beauty, so much so that he regarded himself to be far superior to all in that respect. It is because of this fault of his that today Nakula has fallen down. My advice to you, my dear brother, is that we must reconcile with these losses and walk on, because everyone has to endure the consequences of faults committed in the past."

11.9 तांस्तु प्रपतितान् दृष्ट्वा पाण्डवः श्वेतवाहनः ।
पपात शोकसन्तप्तस्ततो नु परवीरहा ॥ 17.2.18

tamstu prapatitan dristva pandavah svetavahanah
papata sokasantaptastato nu paraviraha

—17.2.18

Simple meaning—After some time, Arjuna, who had earned so much fame as a warrior (and whose chariot used to be pulled by white steeds), suddenly lost his concentration and fell down, because he was stuck with grief at the loss of Draupadi, Sahadeva and Nakula.

तस्मिंस्तु पुरुषव्याघ्रे पतिते शक्रतेजसि ।
म्रियमाणे दुराधर्षे भीमो राजानमब्रवीत् ॥ 17.2.19

tasmimstu purusavyaghre patite sakratejasi
mriyamane duradharse bhimo rajanambravit

—17.2.19

Simple meaning—Seeing that Arjuna, who was like a lion among men and who had the energy of Indra, has fallen down and was on the point of death, Bhima once more put a question to Yudhisthira (as he had done after the fall of Draupadi, Sahadeva and Nakula).

अनृतं न स्मराम्यस्य स्वैरेष्वपि महात्मनः ।
अथ कस्य विकारोऽयं येनायं पतितो भुवि ॥ 17.2.20

anritam na smaramyasya svairesvapi mahatmanah
atha kasya vikaroyam yenayam patito bhuvi
—17.2.20

Simple meaning—Bhima asked Yudhisthira, "O learned brother, as far as I know, this brother of ours (i.e. Arjuna) was a high-souled man; in fact, I do not recollect any untruth uttered by him, even in jest. Can you please tell me what wrong he could have committed, because of which he has fallen down on earth."

युधिष्ठिर उवाच

एकाह्ना निर्दहेयं वै शत्रूनित्यर्जुनोऽब्रवीत् ।
न च तत् कृतवानेष शूरमानी ततोऽपतत् ॥ 17.2.21
अवमेने धनुर्ग्राहानेष सर्वांश्च फाल्गुनः ।
तथा चैतन्न तु तथा कर्तव्यं भूतिमिच्छता ॥ 17.2.22

yudhisthira uvaca
ekahna nirdaheyam vai satrunityarjunobravit
na ca tat kritavanesa suramani tatopatat
—17.2.21

avamene dhanurgrahanesa sarvamsca phalgunah
tatha caitanna tu tatha kartavyam bhutimicchata
—17.2.22

Simple meaning—Yudhisthira replied to Bhima, "My dear brother, I agree with what you said about Arjuna, but I have to point out one fault of his, viz. that he overestimated his capability; he declared that he would destroy all our enemies in a single day, but he was not able to do that. Hence he has fallen down. But we can learn a lesson from Arjuna's experience. He did not show proper regard to other wielders of bows. The lesson to be learnt is that no one seeking one's own welfare should disregard others."

11.10 इत्युक्त्वा प्रस्थितो राजा भीमोऽथ निपपात ह ।
पतितश्चाब्रवीद् भीमो धर्मराजं युधिष्ठिरम् ॥ 17.2.23

ityuktva prasthito raja bhimotha nipapata ha
patitascabravid bhimo dharmarajam yudhisthiram
—17.2.23

Simple meaning—Having said so, Yudhisthira walked on. Then suddenly Bhima fell down. Realizing that he too has fallen like others, Bhima put his final question to Yudhisthira (as he had done after the fall of Draupadi, Sahadeva, Nakula, and Arjuna).

भो भो राजन्नवेक्षस्व पतितोऽहं प्रियस्तव ।
किं निमित्तं च पतनं ब्रूहि मे यदि वेत्थ ह ॥ 17.2.24

bho bho rajannaveksasva patitoham priyastava
kim nimittam ca patanam bruhi me yadi vettha ha
—17.2.24

Simple meaning—Bhima asked Yudhisthira, "O learned brother, please look towards me. Although I am so dear to you, I too have fallen down. If you know the reason for my fall, please let me know."

युधिष्ठिर उवाच
अतिभुक्तं च भवता प्राणेन च विकत्थसे ।
अनवेक्ष्य परं पार्थ तेनासि पतितः क्षितौ ॥ 17.2.25

yudhisthira uvaca
atibhuktam ca bhavata pranena ca vikatthase
anaveksya param partha tenasi patitah ksitau
—17.2.25

Simple meaning—Yudhisthira replied to Bhima, "My dear brother, you are so dear to me, but I have to point out the reason for your fall. You were a great eater so much so that you did not leave enough for others. Also you used to boast of your strength."

11.11 इत्युक्त्वा तं महाबाहुर्जगामानवलोकयन् ।
श्वाप्येकोऽनुययौ यस्ते बहुशः कीर्तितो मया ॥ 17.2.26

ityuktva tam mahabahurjagamanavalokayan
svapyekonuyayau yaste bahusah kirtito maya
—17.2.26

Simple meaning—Having replied to Bhima's last question, Yudhisthira walked on, without looking back. At this point he had only one companion, viz. the dog that walked behind him. (The special role of the dog will soon be clear).

11.12 ततः सन्नादयञ्शक्रो दिवं भूमिं च सर्वशः ।
रथेनोपययौ पार्थमारोहेत्यब्रवीच्च तम् ॥ 17.3.1
tatah sannadayamsakro divam bhumim ca sarvasah
rathenopayayau parthamarohetyabravicca tam
—17.3.1

Simple meaning—Suddenly Indra's chariot arrived there, the sound of which filled the skies and the worlds. Indra greeted Yudhisthira and said, "Welcome, O Partha, please ascend this chariot so that I can take you to heaven."

11.13 स्वभ्रातॄन् पतितान् दृष्ट्वा धर्मराजो युधिष्ठिरः ।
अब्रवीच्छोकसंतप्तः सहस्राक्षमिदं वचः ॥ 17.3.2
svabhratrin patitan dristva dharmarajo yudhisthirah
abravicchokasantaptah sahasraksamidam vacah
—17.3.2

Simple meaning—The righteous - souled Yudhisthira was, at that time, filled with grief because his wife and four brothers were no longer with him since they had fallen on the way. With a heavy heart, Yudhisthira spoke to Indra.

युधिष्ठिर उवाच
भ्रातरः पतिता मेऽत्र गच्छेयुस्ते मया सह ।
न विना भ्रातृभिः स्वर्गमिच्छे गन्तुं सुरेश्वर ॥ 17.3.3
सुकुमारी सुखार्हा च राजपुत्री पुरंदर।
सास्माभिः सह गच्छेत तद् भवाननुमन्यताम् ॥ 17.3.4
yudhisthira uvaca
bhratarah patita metra gaccheyuste maya saha
na vina bhratribhih svargamicche gantum suresvara
—17.3.3

sukumari sukharha ca rajaputri purandara
sasmabhih saha gaccheta tad bhavananumanyatam
—17.3.4

Simple meaning—Yudhisthira said to Indra, "O chief of heaven, I do not want to go to heaven alone. So, if you want to take me to heaven, please arrange that my wife and brothers, who have fallen on the way, may accompany me. Having been an excellent princess, my wife deserves heavenly comforts. Please allow that she may accompany me and my brothers to heaven."

11.14 शक्र उवाच

भ्रातृन् द्रक्ष्यसि स्वर्गे त्वमग्रतस्त्रिदिवं गतान् ।
कृष्णया सहितान् सर्वान् मा शुचो भरतर्षभ ॥ 17.3.5
निक्षिप्य मानुषं देहं गतास्ते भरतर्षभ ।
अनेन त्वं शरीरेण स्वर्गे गन्ता न संशयः ॥ 17.3.6

sakra uvaca
bhratrin draksyasi svarge tvamagratastridivam gatan
krisnaya sahitan sarvan ma suco bharatarsabha
—17.3.5
niksipya manusam deham gataste bharatarsabha
anena tvam sarirena svarge ganta na samsayah
—17.3.6

Simple meaning—Indra said to Yudhisthira, "O chief of the Bharatas, your brothers and Draupadi are already in heaven, and you will see them there. You need not have any worry on their account. The only difference between you and them is, that they have given up their human body prior to reaching heaven, but you have not."

11.15 युधिष्ठिर उवाच

अयं श्वा भूतभव्येश भक्तो मां नित्यमेव ह ।
स गच्छेत मया सार्धमानृशंस्या हि मे मति : ॥ 17.3.7

yudhisthira uvaca
ayam sva bhutabhavyesa bhakto mam nityameva ha
sa gaccheta maya sardhamanrisamsya hi me matih
—17.3.7

Simple meaning—Yudhisthira said to Indra, "O Lord of the past and the present, this dog is a great devotee of mine. He has been walking with me, so please allow that he may accompany me to heaven. In my opinion, absence of cruelty is most important."

11.16 शक्र उवाच
अमर्त्यत्वं मत्समत्वं च राजन्
श्रियं कृत्स्नां महतीं चैव सिद्धिम् ।
सम्प्राप्तोऽद्य स्वर्गसुखानि च त्वं
त्यज श्वानं नात्र नृशंसमस्ति ॥ 17.3.8

sakra uvaca
amartyatvam matsamatvam ca rajan
sriyam kritsnam mahatim caiva siddhim
sampraptodya svargasukhani ca tvam
tyaja svanam natra nrisamsamasti

—17.3.8

Simple meaning—Indra said to Yudhisthira, "O King, today you have achieved so many great things, viz. immortality, a status equal to mine, vast prosperity, big success, and all the joys of heaven. So leave this dog. There is no cruelty in that."

11.17 युधिष्ठिर उवाच
अनार्यमार्येण सहस्रनेत्र
शक्यं कर्तुं दुष्करमेतदार्य ।
मा मे श्रिया संगमनं तयास्तु
यस्याः कृते भक्तजनं त्यजेयम् ॥ 17.3.9
yudhisthira uvaca
anaryamaryena sahasranetra
sakyam kartum duskarametadarya
ma me sriya sangamanam tayastu
yasyah krite bhaktajanam tyajeyam

—17.3.9

Simple meaning—Yudhisthira said to Indra, "O righteous - souled chief having a vision of thousand eyes, you know how difficult it is for a person of righteous mentality to do some thing which is unrighteous. On my part, I would never wish to have that prosperity for the sake of which I shall have to cast off one that is devoted to me."

11.18 शक्र उवाच

स्वर्गे लोके श्ववतां नास्ति स्थानं
इष्टापूर्तं क्रोधवशा हरन्ति ।
ततो विचार्य क्रियतां धर्मराज
त्यज श्वानं नात्र नृशंसमस्ति ॥ 17.3.10

sakra uvca
svarge loke svavatam nasti sthanam
istapurtam krodhavasa haranti
tato vicarya kriyatam dharmaraja
tyaja svanam natra nrisamsamasti

—17.3.10

Simple meaning—Indra said to Yudhisthira, "O rightesous - souled king, I appreciate your wish to avoid cruelty, but I also have to observe a rule that persons with dogs are not allowed entry into heaven. Therefore, please take a decision after careful consideration. My advice to you again is to leave this dog, because there is no cruelty in that."

11.19 युधिष्ठिर उवाच

भक्तत्यागं प्राहुरत्यन्तपापं
तुल्यं लोके ब्रह्मवध्याकृतेन ।
तस्मान्नाहं जातु कथंचनाद्य
त्यक्ष्याम्येनं स्वसुखार्थी महेन्द्र ॥ 17.3.11

yudhisthira uvaca
bhaktatyagam prahuratyantapapam
tulyam loke brahmavadhyakritena
tasmannaham jatu kathancanadya
tyaksyamyenam svasukharthi mahendra

—17.3.11

Simple meaning—Yudhisthira said to Indra, "O great Indra, it has been said by Rishis that the sin caused by the abandonment of a devotee is as serious as the killing of a scholar, and that it will haunt one for ever. Hence, my decision is that, for the sake of my own happiness, I shall not abandon this dog today, under any circumstances."

भीतं भक्तं नान्यदस्तीति चार्तं
प्राप्तं क्षीणं रक्षणे प्राणलिप्सुम्।
प्राणत्यागादप्यहं नैव मोक्तुं
यतेयं वै नित्यमेतद् व्रतं मे ॥ 17.3.12

bhitam bhaktam nanyadastiti cartam
praptam ksinam raksane pranalipsum
pranatyagadapyaham naiva moktum
yateyam vai nityametad vratam me

—17.3.12

Simple meaning—Yudhisthira added, "Not only today, for I have always firmly stood by this principle, viz. that, even at the cost of my own life, I shall not abandon one who is terrified, or one who is devoted to me, or one who is in distress, or one who seeks my protection, saying that I have no other person to help me."

11.20 शक्र उवाच

त्यक्त्वा भ्रातृन् दयितां चापि कृष्णां
प्राप्तो लोकः कर्मणा स्वेन वीर।
श्वानं चैनं न त्यजसे कथं नु
त्यागं कृत्स्नं चास्थितो मुह्यसेऽद्य ॥ 17.3.14

sakra uvaca

tyaktva bhratrin dayitam capi krisnam
prapto lokah karmana svena vira
svanam cainam na tyajase katham nu
tyagam kritsnam casthito muhyasedya

—17.3.14

Simple meaning—Indra said to Yudhisthira, "O brave and kind soul, please look at the situation dispassionately. You abandoned your brothers and Draupadi, but that did not keep you away from heaven which you earned by your own good deeds. So why can't you abandon this dog? In fact, it seems as if you gave up everything and now got stuck with this dog in attachment caused due to ignorance."

11.21 युधिष्ठिर उवाच

न विद्यते संधिरथापि विग्रहो
मृतैर्मर्त्यैरिति लोकेषु निष्ठा ।
न ते मया जीवयितुं हि शक्याः
ततस्त्यागस्तेषु कृतो न जीवताम् ॥ 17.3.15

na vidyate sandhirathapi vigraho
mritairmartyairiti lokesu nistha
na te maya jivayitum hi sakyah
tatastyagastesu krito na jivatam

—17.3.15

Simple meaning—Yudhisthira said to Indra, " O kind soul, please look at my situation sympathetically. It is well-known in all the worlds that there is neither friendship nor enmity with those that are dead. When my brothers and Draupadi died, I was unable to revive them. Hence is was at that point that I abandoned them. I did not, however, abandon them as long as they were alive."

भीतिप्रदानं शरणागतस्य
स्त्रिया वधो ब्राह्मणस्वापहारः ।
मित्रद्रोहस्तानि चत्वारि शक्र
भक्तत्यागश्चैव समो मतो मे ॥ 17.3.16

bhitipradanam saranagatasya
striya vadho brahmanasvapaharah
mitradrohastani catvari sakra
bhaktatyagascaiva samo mato me

—17.3.16

Simple meaning—Yudhisthira added, "In my opinion, the abandonment of a devotee (who is still alive) is the worst sin, because this by itself is as bad as the following four sinful acts put together -- to frighten one who has sought protection, to slay a woman, to steal what belongs to a brahmin, and to do harm to a friend."

11.22 तद् धर्मराजस्य वचो निशम्य
धर्मस्वरूपी भगवानुवाच ।
युधिष्ठिरं प्रीतियुक्तो नरेन्द्रं
श्लक्ष्णैर्वाक्यैः संस्तवसम्प्रयुक्तैः ॥ 17.3.17

tad dharmarajasya vaco nisamya
dharmasvarupi bhagavanuvaca
yudhisthiram pritiyukto narendram
slaksanairvakyaih samstavasamprayuktaih

—17.3.17

Simple meaning—Upon hearing such divinely inspired words of Yudhisthira, the dog became transformed into his real form i.e. Lord of Dharma. The drama which was enacted jointly by Indra and Lord of Dharma, now became clear to Yudhisthira also.

11.23 This is how Yudhisthira obtained complete success in achieving a glorious end for his wife and brothers (after they had fallen, while walking towards heaven). Yudhisthira's refusal to give up his lokasamgraha-principles (aimed at doing good to all)[1], under any circumstances, proved to be the key to his success.

Chapter 12

How Pandavas Helped Matsya Kingdom Face Calamities

12.1 Virata Parva (i.e. Parva number Four) provides a good example of a state which, by itself, would have succumbed to aggressors, but which with the help of the Pandavas, was able to save itself from calamities. The name of this state was Matsya, and the name of the Matsya King was Virata. The capital city of Matsya kingdom was the place where the five Pandavas, and their wife Draupadi, spent one year, disguising themselves so skilfully that secret service agents of the Kauravas gave the following report to Duryodhana at Hastinapur (the capital city of Kauravas)–

न हि विद्मो गतिं तेषां
वासं चापि महात्मनाम् ॥ 4.25.17

na hi vidmo gatim tesam
vasam capi mahatmanam

—*4.25.17*

Simple meaning—Secret service agents told Duryodhana about the Pandavas – "We could discover, neither their track, nor their present abode."

12.2 Sitting with Duryodhana at that time, was Susharma, King of Trigarta state. The two neighboring states, Trigarta and Matsya, had a long history of mutual conflict. In their last encounter, Matsya's commander-in-cheif, Kichaka, had proved to be a cruel tormentor. Susharma, therefore, paid special attention to the secret service agents' words that specifically referred to Kichaka's death.

येन त्रिगर्ता निहता बलेन महता नृप ।
सूतेन राज्ञो मत्स्यस्य कीचकेन बलीयसा ॥ 4.25.20
स हतः पतितः शेते गन्धर्वैर्निशि भारत ।
अदृश्यमानैर्दुष्टात्मा भ्रातृभिः सह सोदरैः ॥ 4.25.21

yena trigarta nihata balena mahata nripa
sutena rajno matsyasya kicakena baliyasa
—4.25.20

sa hatah patitah sete gandharvairnisi bharata
adrisyamanairdustatma bhratribhih saha sodaraih
—4.25.21

Simple meaning—The secret service agents reported to Duryodhana at Hastinapur, "The evil commander, Kichaka, who was the brother-in-law of the Matsya king Virata, and who had earlier killed so many Trigarta-residents, is now dead. They say that, since Kichaka's behavior towards the new maid servant Sairandhri was improper, some invisible Gandharva killed him and his brothers too, at night."

12.3 After listening to the agents as well as to Susharma, the evil-minded Duryodhana guessed (correctly)–

तत्राहं कीचकं मन्ये भीमसेनेन मारितम् ।
सैरन्ध्रीं द्रौपदीं मन्ये नात्र कार्या विचारणा ॥ 4.29.22

tatraham kicakam manye bhimasenena maritam
sairandhrim draupadim manye natra karya vicarana
—4.29.22

Simple meaning—Duryodhana said, "I think that invisible Gandharva who killed the mighty Kichaka is Bhima, because no one else could possibly do so. And that new maid servant Sairandhri, who got Kichaka killed, is Draupadi in disguise."

12.4 As a follow-up of the above, Duryodhana and Susharma jointly hatched a plot, to attack the Matsya kingdom, from two different directions, and on two consecutive days.

Susharma said that he will launch his attack from the south, on the seventh day of the month. The Matsya king Virata will then try to offer resistance with the help of a new commander-in-cheif (who is unlikely to be as great a commander as Kichaka was). In order to inflict a crippling blow on Matsya kingdom, it was decided by Duryodhana that he will launch his attack from the north, on the eighth day of the month.

12.5 When Susharma attacked Matsya kingdom, the initial results were what he had expected. Weakened by the death of Kichaka, the Matsya army was unable to face the invading forces (i.e the Trigarta army).

12.6 But the Pandavas, living in disguise in the Matsya kingdom, felt that they should help Virata (the Matsya king) at this catastrophic moment. Yudhisthira, therefore, spoke to Bhima.

युधिष्ठिर उवाच

उषिताः स्म सुखं सर्वे सर्वकामैः सुपूजिताः ।
भीमसेन त्वया कार्या तस्य वासस्य निष्कृतिः ॥ 4.33.13

yudhisthira uvaca
usitah sma sukham sarve sarvakamaih supujitah
bhimasena tvaya karya tasya vasasya niskritih

—4.33.13

Simple meaing—Yudhisthira said, "My dear Bhima, you know how grateful we are to King Virata – he has given us shelter and we have spent one year comfortably in disguise. Now is the time for us to do something in return."

12.7 Since Virata did not know that his cook, Ballava, was Bhima in disguise, he was completely taken aback when he saw that Ballava, reversing the trend of the battle, overpowered Susharma. At that moment, Yudhisthira intervened.

युधिष्ठिर उवाच

तं राजा प्राहसन् दृष्ट्वा
मुच्यतां वै नराधमः ॥ 4.33.58

yudhisthira uvaca
tam raja prahasan dristva
mucyatam vai naradhamah

—4.33.58

Simple meaning—Yudhisthira said to Bhima, "You have accomplished the task that I assigned to you. But don't kill Susharma although he had committed aggression against Matsya kingdom."

Then Bhima reprimanded Susharma

जीवितुं चेच्छसे मूढ हेतुं ते गदतः शृणु ॥ 4.33.59
दासोऽस्मीति त्वया वाच्यं संसत्सु च सभासु च ।
एवं ते जीवितं दद्यामेष युद्धजितो विधिः ॥ 4.33.60

jivitum cecchase mudha hetum te gadatah srinu

—4.33.59

dasosmiti tvaya vacyam samsatsu ca sabhasu ca
evam te jivitam dadyamesa yuddhajito vidhih

—4.33.60

Simple meaning—Bhima said to Susharma, "Only foolish kings commit aggression against neighbouring states. But we cannot let such aggression succeed. Furthermore, our policy is, to set in motion a process to put an end to aggressive practices. Go and declare to the assembly of people's representatives in your (Trigarta) state that you have learnt this lesson and that all the people should support this new policy of non-aggression."

12.8 Repulsing aggression on the southern front was a big relief. However, neither Virata nor Yudhisthira had any idea at that time that Matsya state was facing another aggression on the northern front. As already agreed to, between Duryodhana and Susharma, the aggression in the north was committed by the Kaurava forces.

12.9 Since Virata and his army had gone to defend the southern front, the responsibility of facing the aggression in the north fell on Prince Uttar. Although outwardly he spoke words of bravery, Uttar knew that the only thing that he could possibly do was to surrender.

नोत्सहे कुरुभिर्योद्धुं रोमहर्षं हि पश्य मे ॥ 4.38.10
त्रिगर्तान् मे पिता यातः शून्ये सम्प्रणिधाय माम् ।
सर्वां सेनामुपादाय न मे सन्तीह सैनिकाः ॥ 4.38.17
प्रतियोद्धुं न शक्यामि निवर्तस्व बृहन्नले ॥ 4.38.18

notsahe kurubhiryoddhum romaharsam hi pasya me
—4.38.10

trigartan me pita yatah sunye sampranidhaya mam
sarvam senamupadaya na me santiha sainikah
—4.38.17

pratiyoddhum na sakyami nivartasva brihannale
—4.38.18

Simple meaning—Uttar explained his predicament to Brihannala (without knowing that Brihannala, the dance teacher, was Arjuna in disguise), "My father took the army to the south, to fight against Susharma's forces, so I am practically alone to face Duryodhana's army in the north. I am nervous and have no enthusiasm to fight. Therefore, Brihannala, let us take our chariot away from the battlefield."

12.10 Realizing the gravity of the situation, Arjuna transferred to himself, the responsibility of facing the Kaurava army.

अर्जुन उवाच
यदि नोत्सहे योद्धुं शत्रुभिः शत्रुकर्षण ।
एहि मे त्वं हयान् यच्छ युद्धमानस्य शत्रुभिः ॥ 4.38.46

arjuna uvaca
yadi notsahe yoddhum satrubhih satrukarsana
ehi me tvam hayan yaccha yuddhamanasya satrubhih
—4.38.46

Simple meaning—Arjuna said to Prince Uttar, "If you have no enthusiasm to fight, let me take charge of fighting because we cannot let the aggressor destroy our kingdom. You become my charioteer."

12.11 What Bhima had achieved on the southern front, was repeated by Arjuna on the northern front. In this way, Matsya Kingdom (because of Pandavas' help) was able to face both the calamities successfully.

> मत्स्यराज्यस्य सामर्थ्यमपर्याप्तं रक्षणार्थम् ।
> पाण्डवानां बलं प्राप्य त्वापद्मुक्तिः सुलभा हि ।
> उत्तरा मत्स्यराज्यस्य भार्या चार्जुनपुत्रस्य ॥ ४.७२.२२
>
> *matsyarajyasya samarthyamaparyaptam raksanartham*
> *pandavanam balam prapya tvapadmuktih sulabha hi*
> *uttara matsyarajyasya bharya carjunaputrasya*
>
> —*4.72.22*

Simple meaning—Matsya Kingdom, by itself, was not strong enough to protect itself. However, with the support of the Pandavas, the Matsyas became strong enough to face two calamities, that stuck them, on two consecutive days, and at two different locations.

12.12 The happiest outcome of the mutual trust (between the Matsyas and the Pandavas) was, that the Matsya Princess Uttara[1] became the wife of Abhimanyu (Arjuna's son). The son of the newly wed couple (named Parikshita) subsequently succeeded Yudhisthira on the throne (because all the sons of the Pandavas were killed in the Mahabharata war).

Part III

Summary

Chapter 13

Summary of Parts I and II and Concluding Remarks

13.1 Due to one reason or the other, most of the Mahabharata - studies published prior to 9/11/2001 concentrated attention on the first half of the text, that is, presented the Mahabharata as "a book of war". However, recent studies have shifted attention from the first to the second half of the text, that is, viewed the Mahabharata as "a book of peace".

13.2 The main source of peace - oriented studies is Shanti Parva, which, for purposes of this book, includes Anusasana Parva (which is a continuation of Shanti Parva). Apad - dharma (dealing with the question 'How to face calamities') is one of the three parts of Shanti Parva, the other two parts being Raja - dharma and Moksa - dharma. Messages of Apad - dharma, as in Shanti Parva as a whole, are given mainly with the help of stories. Some of the stories of Raja - dharma and Moksa- dharma also deal with the question 'How to face calamities'. So, in Part I of this book, we have made use of stories from all the three parts of Shanti Parva. In Part II of the book, we have included stories from Parvas other than Shanti Parva (i.e. stories which deal with the question 'How to face calamities'). In all, ten stories are given (in Parts I and II combined), out of which seven are related to individual level calamities (in chapters 3, 4, 5, 8, 9, 10, 11), two are related to state level calamities (in chapters 6, 12), and one is related to global level calamity (in chapter 7).

13.3 The main contribution of this book is that, based on the numerous stories of the Mahabharata, ten sources of strength (needed to face any calamity) have been identified. Elaboration of the role of each source of strength gives rise to messages of Apad - dharma. Readers will notice that these messages are non - denominational, and have universal applicability. Readers will also notice that, although the Mahabharata is an ancient text, its messages are relevant even today, and deserve to be read with an open mind.

13.4 Although stories related to personal, state, and global level calamities are presented in separate chapters, no such separation can be made in regard to messages that may be relevant to different levels of calamities, because these messages overlap quite a bit. The overall message of Apad - dharma is that every calamity should be faced intelligently, avoiding a foolhardy approach. Strength of head and heart is given precedence over physical strength, without undervaluing the latter. In fact, the following ten sources of strength constitute the general framework out of which the applicability of a particular source to a specific calamity depends on a case - by - case assessment :-

(i) Heart हृदय (hridaya)

(ii) Prayer प्रार्थना (prarthana)

(iii) Self-purification आत्मशुद्धि (atmasuddhi)

(iv) Joint effort संघात (sanghata)

(v) Unbreakable relationship भेदमुक्ति (bhedamukti)

(vi) Intellect बुद्धि (buddhi)

(vii) Vocal skill वाक् (vak)

(viii) Skill in action कर्मकौशल (karmakausala)

(ix) Change of priorities प्राथमिकता परिवर्तन (prathamikata parivartana)

(x) Steadfastness धृति (dhriti)

13.5 Heart हृदय (hridaya)

Apad-dharma says that a faint-hearted person who starts crying at the arrival of a calamity, is inherently incapable of facing that calamity. If you lose heart, you succumb to the calamity even before it strikes you. You might even commit suicide. Therefore, don't let will power abandon you. Don't feel that there is no hope of success. At this early stage, you cannot possibly identify the door to safety. But a brave heart will give you hope that a "door of no-door" does exist, although you can not see it. Your immediate response should be to keep the urge to make effort.

13.6 Prayer प्रार्थना (prarthana)

The purpose underlying prayer, according to Apad-dharma, is not to ask for easy victory (handed over to me without any effort on my part), but rather to ask for strength needed to face the calamity. "Strength" includes physical and moral strength for which Shanti Parva recommends the practice of yoga, pranayama and meditation, and consumption of healthy, vegetarian food.

13.7 Self -purification आत्मशुद्धि (atmasuddhi)

The role of self - purification is particularly important if one's own mistakes have contributed to the occurrence of the calamity. Apad - dharma points out that the process of self - purification consists of two steps -

(a) Repentance, and strengthening of self - discipline

(b) Determination that old mistakes will not be repeated, and also that even unpleasant action will be gladly undertaken, if needed to rectify those mistakes. The importance of self - purification (or reform) is brought out in Gautami's story (in chapter 3).

13.8 Joint effort संघात (sanghata)

Apad - dharma gives two crucial pieces of advice -

(a) It is not advisable to face the calamity "alone".

(b) It is not advisable to face several enemies, all at the same time.

To implement (a), one should look for supporters.

To implement (b), one should try to make peace with at least one of the enemies.

A comparative assessment of one's own strength, and that of the ememies, is essential. The role of 'sanghata' (joint effort) is to alter the situation in one's favour. Apad - dharma stresses the need to avoid an "unequal battle in which one is bound to lose" (that would be like committing suicide). The importance of "sanghata" is brought out in two stories (chapters 5 and 12)

13.9 Unbreakable relationship भेदमुक्ति (bhedamukti)

Apad - dharma says that the inherent strength of a state depends on the nature of relationship that exists among important subgroups that together sustain the state. The calamity that a state faces, occurs more often due to internal problems, as compared to external causes. The main cause of destruction of a state is 'lack of internal unity or team spirit'. What is needed is 'harmonious relationship and unity of purpose'. The harmonious relationship has to be unbreakable and unbribable, and that makes the state 'unconquerable'. That is why 'bhedamukti' (unbreakable relationship) and 'apadmukti' (calamity - free existence)are practically synonymous expressions in Apad-dharma. Relevant stories are given in Chapter 6.

13.10 Intellect बुद्धि (buddhi)

Apad - dharma uses the expressions 'buddhi', 'prajna' and 'medha' as practically interchangeable (and, in the present context, the English word 'intellect' covers all of them). This source of strength is given special recognition, in the context of facing calamities at all levels. Supporters who give the right advice contribute the most to the effectiveness of joint effort.

Right intellect studies the situation scientifically - comparative strength of both sides in the conflict, how to negotiate a peace treaty if it is in one's interest, etc. - and then works out the best possible plan for success (which may include a peace treaty with at least one of the enemies).

Illustrative stories (or historical narratives) bringing out the importance of intellect are given in chapters 5, 7, and 10.

13.11 Vocal skill वाक् (vak)

Since Shanti Parva's overall recommendation is to face calamities peacefully, the problems are to resolved in conference halls, and not on the battle field. Therefore, vocal skill is very important. According to Apad - dharma, vocal skill includes (a) polite speach, (b) speaking what is relevant, (c) speech that is free from ill will, (d) truthful speech and (e) speech that uses carefully chosen words.

The importance of vocal skill is brought out in three stories (in chapters 4, 8, and 9).

13.12 Skill in action कर्मकौशल (karmakausala)

Shanti Parva uses the expressions 'karmakausala' and 'daksya' interchangeably. Skill in action includes not only efficiency but also the desire to do good to all, that is, lokasamgraha. Shanti Parva has explained the concept of lokasamgraha from ten angles, one of which is 'mutual indebtedness'. Human beings should recognize that they are always indebted to society (for having brought them up and for having developed their capability). To apply their capability and work for doing good to the society, that is, to have a sense of social responsibility, is the right way to repay their debt.

The importance of skill in action (which includes lokasamgraha) is brought out in three stories (in chapters 7, 11, and 12)

13.13 Change of priorities प्राथमिकता परिवर्तन (prathamikata parivartana)

Shanti Parva says that the traditional Varnashrama - dharma is meant for times of peace, but needs to be adjusted for times of crisis. Similarly, the traditional recommendation about having four goals of life (artha, kama, dharma, moksa) needs to be modified, because all the citizens of the state must give priority to facing the calamity successfully (which becomes the single goal of life in times of crisis). In order to face the crisis successfully, the state requires that all the citizens willingly accept the principle of change of priorities. Chapters 6, 7, and 9 provide illustrative material on this.

13.14 Steadfastness धृति (dhriti)

Apad-dharma says that facing a serious calamity must be viewed as a long-term effort, in the course of which, ups and downs are bound to come. At all stages of the struggle, in order to make steady progress towards the attainment of the objective, the Karmayogin will require (a) steadfastness, (b) skill in action, (c) co-ordination, (d) updating of knowledge, (e) patience, (f) enthusiasm, and (g) willingness to make adjustments, according to changes in time, place and circumstances, so as not to become obsolete and ineffective. The point (d) means that education and training have an important role in facing calamities. The point (g) means that acceptance of the 'desh-kala-patra' doctrine becomes an important source of strength when the struggle involved in facing a calamity goes on and on. Medhavi's story in chapter 7 provides illustrative material on the points specified in this para, particularly in the context of a global calamity.

13.15 This completes a summarization of Apad-dharma's messages on 'how to face calamities' (arising out of chapter 2). From chapter 3 to chapter 12, there are ten stories which provide illustrative material vis-a-vis those messages. Reference to all these stories has already been made in the summary given above. Therefore, a separate, story-by-story 'summary' does not seem to be necessary - it might make this chapter too long.

Concluding remarks

13.16 Apad-dharma's answer to the question 'How to face any calamity', is based on promoting feelings of strength, courage, confidence and hopefulness. These feelings are, in turn, based on a scientific analysis of (a) why the calamity has arrived, and (b) relative strength of forces, for or against us. If the calamity has arrived due to our own mistakes, then we have to be willing to rectify those mistakes. Whatever might be the causes that have brought the calamity at our door, a plan to eliminate those causes must be drawn up, as a preventive measure to avert future calamities.

13.17 A scientific analysis of 'relative strength of forces, for or against us' is most important. Apad-dharma insists that a conflict-flare-up must be avoided when the 'forces against us' are stronger than 'forces for us' because such a step would be suicidal. In order to strengthen 'forces for us' we need to find supporters. At the same time, in order to weaken 'forces against us', we need to try to make peace with at least one of the 'forces against us.'

13.18 In view of the above, the Apad - dharma approach can be characterized as a scientific and success-oriented approach. Furthermore, since Apad-dharma is presented in the Mahabharata as an integral part of Shanti Parva, the Apad-dharma approach is a peace - oriented approach. Gandhian scholars should study in detail, points of similarity between the Apad-dharma approach and the Gandhian approach. The recent history of India can provide a good example of similarity, because, viewing the 'lack of independence' as a state - level calamity, the Apad-dharma approach (in the early twentieth century) could have (conceptually) suggested an initiative similar to the Gandhian Satyagraha. An amalgamation of the two approaches (in the 21st century) can lead to the preparation of a detailed plan for world peace, which can be submitted to the United Nations.

APPENDIX

Apad-dharma's Story of Three Fish

नातिगाधे जलाधारे सुहृदः कुशलास्त्रयः ।
प्रभूतमत्स्ये कौन्तेय बभूवुः सहचारिणः ॥ 12.137.3

natigadhe jaladhare suhridah kusalastrayah
prabhutamatsye kaunteya babhuvuh sahacarinah
—12.137.3

Simple meaning—A large number of fish lived in a pond that was not very deep. For this story, we concentrate our attention on three fish, who lived there as close friends.

तत्रैको दीर्घकालज्ञ उत्पन्नप्रतिभोऽपरः ।
दीर्घसूत्रश्च तत्रैकस्त्रयाणां सहचारिणाम् ॥ 12.137.4

tatraiko dirghakalajna utpannapratibhoparah
dirghasutrasca tatraikastrayanam sahacarinam
—12.137.4

Simple meaning—Although the three fish were close friends, their mentality was quite different. One liked to take protective and preventive action in advance. The second fish was confident that his presence of mind will save him at the last moment. The third fish did not want to take any action at all.

कदाचित् तं जलस्थायं मत्स्यबन्धाः समन्ततः ।
निस्रावयामासुरथो निम्नेषु विविधैर्मुखैः ॥ 12.137.5

kadacit tam jalasthayam matsyabandhah samantatah
nisravayamasuratho nimnesu vividhairmukhaih
—12.137.5

Simple meaning—One day some fishermen began to bail out the water of that pond to a lower ground through diverse outlets.

प्रक्षीयमाणं तं दृष्ट्वा जलस्थायं भयागमे ।
अब्रवीद् दीर्घदर्शी तु तावुभौ सुहृदौ तदा ॥ 12.137.6
prakshiyamanam tam dristva jalasthayam bhayagame
abravid dirghadarsi tu tavubhau suhridau tada
—12.137.6

Simple meaning—Beholding the water of the pond gradually decreasing, the fish that liked to take advance action, became aware of the impending danger, and so spoke to his two friends.

इयमापत् समुत्पन्ना सर्वेषां सलिलौकसाम् ।
शीघ्रमन्यत्र गच्छामः पन्था यावन्न दुष्यति ॥ 12.137.7
iyamapat samutpanna sarvesam salilaukasam
sighramanyatra gacchamah pantha yavanna dusyati
—12.137.7

Simple meaning—The far-sighted fish said to his two friends, "A calamity will soon overtake all the fish living in this pond. Let us speedily go to some other pond before our path to safety becomes obstructed."

अनागतमनर्थं हि सुनयैर्यः प्रबाधयेत् ।
स न संशयमाप्नोति रोचतां भो व्रजामहे ॥ 12.137.8
anagatamanartham hi sunayairyah prabadhayet
sa na samsayamapnoti rocatam bho vrajamahe
—12.137.8

Simple meaning—The far-sighted fish added, "My dear friends, I have heard from wise people that the best policy to save yourself from impending danger is to take advance action. I hope you will agree. In that case, all three of us can leave this place now and move on to a safe place."

दीर्घसूत्रस्तु यस्तत्र सोऽब्रवीत् सम्यगुच्यते ।
न तु कार्या त्वरा तावदिति मे निश्चिता मतिः ॥ 12.137.9

dirghasutrastu yastatra sobravit samyagucyate
na tu karya tvara tavaditi me niscita matih

—12.137.9

Simple meaning—In reply to the first fish, the third fish whose policy was not to take any aciton at all, said, "My dear friend, you have spoken nice words. However, I am not going to be moved from my firm policy. So you may go to another pond, but I will stay on here."

अथ सम्प्रतिपत्तिज्ञः प्रावदीद् दीर्घदर्शिनम् ।
प्राप्ते काले न मे किंचिन्न्यायतः परिहास्यते ॥ 12.137.10

atha sampratipattijnah pravadid dirghadarsinam
prapte kale na me kincinnyayatah parihasyate

—12.137.10

Simple meaning—Then the second fish replied to the first fish, "My dear friend, I too have my firm policy, viz. not to take advance action, because my presence of mind will save me at the last moment. So you may move to another pond alone."

एवं श्रुत्वा निराक्रम्य दीर्घदर्शी महामतिः ।
जगाम स्रोतसा तेन गम्भीरं सलिलाशयम् ॥ 12.137.11

evam srutva nirakramya dirghadarsi mahamatih
jagama srotasa tena gambhiram salilasayam

—12.137.11

Simple meaning—After getting the replies from his two friends, the wise fish who believed in taking advance action, had no choice except moving to another pond alone.

ततः प्रसृततोयं तं प्रसमीक्ष्य जलाशयम् ।
बबन्धुर्विविधैर्योगैर्मत्स्यान् मत्स्योपजीविनः ॥ 12.137.12

tatah prasritatoyam tam prasamiksya jalasayam
babandhurvividhairyogairmatsyan matsyopajivinah

—12.137.12

Simple meaning—Seeing that most of the water of that pond had been bailed out, the fishermen started the operation of catching all the fish that were there.

विलोड्यमाने तस्मिंस्तु स्रुततोये जलाशये ।
अगच्छद् बन्धनं तत्र दीर्घसूत्रः सहापरैः ॥ 12.137.13
vilodyamane tasmimstu srutatoye jalasaye
agacchad bandhanam tatra dirghasutrah sahaparaih
—12.137.13

Simple meaning—The fish-catching operation of the fishermen brought sad news to the third fish who had taken no preventive action at all, that is, he was caught along with the other fish.

उद्याने क्रियमाणे तु मत्स्यानां तत्र रज्जुभिः ।
प्रविश्यान्तरमेतेषां स्थितः सम्प्रतिपत्तिमान् ॥ 12.137.14
udyane kriyamane tu matsyanam tatra rajjubhih
pravisyantarametesam sthitah sampratipattiman
—12.137.14

Simple meaning—The second fish, who had confidence in his presence of mind, devised a trick to save himself. When the fishermen began to tie to a long string, the fish that they had caught, the second fish thrust himself into the group of those who had been so tied (although the second fish had not been actually tied).

गृह्यमेव तदुद्यानं गृहीत्वा तं तथैव सः ।
सर्वानेव च तांस्तत्र ते विदुर्ग्रथितानिति ॥ 12.137.15
grihyameva tadudyanam grihitva tam tathaiva sah
sarvaneva ca tamstatra te vidurgrathitaniti
—12.137.15

Simple meaning—The fishermen believed that all the fish attached to the string had been tied (although the second fish, without having been tied, only gave the appearance of having been tied).

ततः प्रक्षाल्यमानेषु मत्स्येषु विपुले जले ।
मुक्त्वा रज्जुं प्रमुक्तोऽसौ शीघ्रं सम्प्रतिपत्तिमान् ॥ 12.137.16
tatah praksalyamanesu matsyesu vipule jale
muktva rajjum pramuktosau sighram samprati pattiman
—12.137.16

Simple meaning—The fishermen took the fish attached to the string, to a pond of deep water, for washing them. The second fish, noted for presence of mind, was able to detach himself from the string, and thus saved himself at the last moment.

अनागतविधाता च प्रत्युत्पन्नमतिश्च यः ।
द्वावेव सुखमेधेते दीर्घसूत्रो विनश्यति ॥ 12.137.20

anagatavidhata ca pratyutmannamatisca yah
dvaveva sukhamedhete dirghasutro vinasyati
—12.137.20

Simple meaning—The conclusion of the story is that, out of the three fish, the most successful in protecting himself was the one who took preventive action in advance. The second fish, who was noted for his presence of mind, was able to save himself at the last moment. But the third fish, who took no action at all, was caught.

Notes

Chapter 1

1. Satya P. Agarwal, Selections from the Mahabharata Reaffirming Gita's Call for the Good of All, Motilal Banarsidass, Delhi, 2002
2. Sitansu S. Chakravarti, Ethics in the Mahabharata-A Philosophical Inquiry for Today, Munshiram Manoharlal, New Delhi, 2006, p. 127
3. Satya P. Agarwal, The World Peace Agenda - Based on Shanti Parva of the Mahabharata, Motilal Banarsidass, Delhi, 2007

Chapter 2

1. For details about Mahabharata's views on vegetarian food, please see Satya P. Agarwal, Selections from the Mahabharata, op. cit., Chapter 17.
2. For details about "desh-kala-patra", please see Satya P. Agarwal, The Gita and Tulsi-Ramayana - Their Common Call for the Good of All, Motilal Banarsidass, Delhi, 2000, Chapter 6.

Chapter 3

1. About the role of education in the context of world peace promotion, please see Satya P. Agarwal, The World Peace Agenda, op. cit., pp. 166-169

Chapter 4

1. For more instances relating to change of heart through non - violence, please see Satya P. Agarwal, The Social Role of the Gita-How and Why, Motilal Banarsidass, Delhi, 1993, pp. 226 - 227

CHAPTER 5

1. For a detailed analysis of "mutual indebtedness", please see Satya P. Agarwal, The Social Role of the Gita, op. cit., pp. 376 – 380.

CHAPTER 6

1. About modern instances of destruction caused by internal conflicts, please see Satya P. Agarwal, The Social Role of the Gita, op.cit., pp. 216-217.

CHAPTER 7

1. For a linkage between sattvika - sukha and lokasamgraha, please see Satya P. Agarwal, The Social Message of the Gita - Symbolized as Lokasamgraha, Motilal Banarsidass, Delhi, 1995, pp. 191 - 192.

CHAPTER 8

1. Vidyut Aklujkar, "Savitri : Old and New", in Arvind Sharma (ed.), Essays on the Mahabharata, E. J. Brill, Laiden, 1991, p. 326

CHAPTER 9

1. Barend A. van Nooten, The Mahabharata attributed to Krishna Dvaipayana Vyasa, Twayne Publishers, New York, 1971, p. 62

CHAPTER 10

1. Barend A. van Nooten, The Mahabharata attributed to Krishna Dvaipayana Vyasa, op.cit., p. 7
2. For a discussion on the role of crisis in the Gita, please see Satya P. Agarwal, The Gita for 21st Century, Motilal Banarsidass, Delhi, 2003, Chapter One.

Chapter 11

1. For a Sanskrit - text devoted to Lokasamgraha, please see Satya P. Agarwal, Lokasamgrahasandesah (in Sanskrit), Motilal Banarsidass, Delhi, 1997

Chapter 12

1. Names of brother and sister were so similar – brother's name was "Uttar" and sister's name was "Uttara".

Index

References are to paragraph numbers, not to pages.